THE LURE OF THE UNKNOWN

The Lure of
the Unknown

Essays on the Strange

by

Algernon Blackwood

Swan River Press
Dublin, Ireland
MMXXII

The Lure of the Unknown
by Algernon Blackwood

Published by
Swan River Press
Dublin, Ireland
December MMXXII

www.swanriverpress.ie
brian@swanriverpress.ie

Introduction and Notes © Mike Ashley
This edition © Swan River Press

Cover design by Meggan Kehrli
from artwork by Chloe Cumming

Set in Garamond by Steve J. Shaw

Published with assistance from Dublin UNESCO
City of Literature and Dublin City Libraries

Paperback Edition
ISBN 978-1-78380-766-6

Swan River Press published
a limited hardback edition of
The Lure of the Unknown in March 2022.

Contents

❧

Hidden Thoughts

Algernon Blackwood (1869-1951) is rightly regarded as one of the pre-eminent writers of supernatural fiction of the first half of the twentieth century—perhaps even the entire century. His ability to take your imagination into the wild places of the world and conjure up manifestations of Nature was unrivalled, and stories such as "The Willows" and "The Wendigo" are regarded as some of the most effective weird fiction ever written.

But of his own innermost thoughts and feelings he kept relatively quiet. He did eventually write an autobiography, though, as the title *Episodes Before Thirty* (1923) reveals, it covers events up to only 1899, when he returned to England after a decade in North America. Even then he was selective, the final paragraph noting:

> Of mystical, psychic, or so-called "occult" experiences, I have purposely said nothing, since these notes have sought to recapture surface adventures only.

He didn't even capture all of those "surface adventures". There is much missing, and often much misleading, in his autobiography, that you can't help but feel there was much that Blackwood did not want to reveal. It took me over twenty years to research his life for my biography *Starlight Man* (2001; revised and expanded 2019) but even then I often felt that I was only scraping the surface.

When I began my research, I was able to borrow an old trunk kept by Sheila Reeves who then represented Blackwood's estate, and this contained a whole jumble of papers, including copies of scripts for his radio and television talks. Some of his talks revealed a little about his inner thoughts, but he was still reticent. His fame in the 1940s, because of his radio and television appearances, meant that he was in demand from magazines and newspapers to write about his experiences, and little by little he opened up, but only so much.

This volume brings together most of the items he wrote that give us a chance to peer into those inner thoughts. They concentrate on his odd, unusual, or strange experiences. Blackwood had, almost from when he became a full-time writer in 1908, contributed articles to periodicals, but these were mostly in the form of travel or nature notes. Some of these even appeared in his story collections, such as "Pines" in *Ten Minute Stories* (1914) or "The Spell of Egypt" in *Tongues of Fire* (1924). But these were mood pieces, reflections upon his appreciation of the world about him.

After he had completed *Episodes Before Thirty*, which at the time he regarded as his final book, he turned to writing more journalism than short stories. This suited his life-style, because he could scribble down thoughts in his notebook regardless of whether he was in the mountains of Switzerland or the deserts of Egypt, or simply sunning himself on the Isle of Capri. The fees he received for his articles were enough to support him in the simple life he liked to live. But he needed subject material and he could only write about the skiing season or the Alpine winds or the flight of birds so many times. So his thoughts turned to other matters such as reincarnation, other dimensions, phobias, and some of his stranger experiences.

The articles included here fall broadly into three categories. There are those which are memories of direct events that Blackwood experienced or those of others whom he knew. Then there are those when he reflects upon certain ideas or concepts. These may also include some personal experiences. Finally, there are three book reviews that he wrote that go beyond simple commentary, and Blackwood uses the space to ruminate on the thoughts these books inspired. One thing these articles do reveal is the wide range of reading and research that Blackwood had undertaken over the years. As such, he was always well informed on whatever subject he chose to write, not just from his reading but also his experiences.

It is disappointing that Blackwood did not write more about his own psychic experiences. There is nothing, for example, about his time as a member of the Hermetic Order of the Golden Dawn apart from what he says in "The Little People & Co." There are just the two articles included here which discuss his research into haunted houses. The first of these, "How I Became Interested in Ghosts", was his very last talk on television and is only preserved because, as he had suffered a stroke, he could no longer extemporise and needed a script. He did consider writing *Episodes After Thirty*, and began dabbling with chapters and notes, but only one of these, "The Fire Body", was published.

His surviving brief notes are infuriating as they hint at so much but never the full story. One such note refers to cases reported to him by Frank Podmore of the Society for Psychical Research, which Blackwood felt were "worth investigating". One of these, called the "Knightsbridge Street Case", he eventually related in that final television talk, but the other, noted below, does not appear in any talk or essay that I know.

Smith-Pigotts in Somersetshire. Obtained permission
from Mrs. S-P in Rome. Figure seen supposed to be
a brother who turned up from France and ousted
the wrongful occupant, his younger brother. Then
disappeared without explanation. This figure always
pointed at certain part of the wall where silver was
kept. Never seen by a woman. Priest from W.s.Mare
tried exorcism ritual, then went to bed. Woke to
see the figure by the bed. Lost consciousness for a
time. When he came to, figure still there, but nearer.
Passed out again till morning. With Edwyn Bevan &
wife we slept a night. Saw nothing.

So we know that Blackwood had other experiences that
he chose not to write about in detail or even hint at in his
essays. But that doesn't mean that his non-fiction writings
have no value at all. The ones collected here reveal his views
on the world and the occult, show his diverse reading and
experiences, and his appreciation of the experiences of
others. He does have a habit of repeating himself across
essays and I'm afraid you will find a few occasions where
an episode is repeated. I did consider how I might edit
these down, but it would have spoiled both the flow
and authenticity of the work, and it does no harm to be
reminded from time to time of the same events. It shows
how important they were to Blackwood.

There are many more essays and reviews by Blackwood
that are not included here. They are mostly thoughts on
nature or extensive travel writings, such as his journey
through the Caucasus which inspired *The Centaur*. His
reviews cover a wide range of subjects, and though I have
included three here, the bulk of these reviews are best
suited to another collection entirely, as are his travel and
nature pieces.

The essays here will show you another side of Blackwood, one that does not appear in *Episodes Before Thirty* but is hinted at in his fiction, because we know that every story he wrote was inspired by something he or a close friend experienced. Blackwood's life was every bit as fascinating as his fiction, and though he was reluctant to say too much about it, these essays allow us a glimpse into that personal world.

Mike Ashley
January 2022

The Lure of the Unknown

Looking Back at Christmas

Christmas, I suppose, is a good moment for private reminiscing; there's a sort of pause in the frantic rush of time, just as there is at New Year.

Looking back over a long stretch, I've found that incidents best remembered are those associated with an emotion. The stronger the emotions of that particular moment, the more vividly they cling. Perhaps the acid associated with a strong emotion bites a deeper groove into what we call the tablets of memory. Such incidents, anyhow, cling like barnacles and refuse to fade.

We'll omit childhood memories, so important to the psychiatrist, usually tiresome and boring, and have a look at incidents of later life. I've found, for instance, that one emotion in particular etches in a deathless memory: horror.

I find certain faces, seen over fifty years ago, as hauntingly clear and vivid as when I first saw them: the faces of quite numerous murderers. Their eyes still look into mine as fixedly as when I was a newspaper reporter in New York in the eighteen-nineties. I could do without these memories, but they never fade. I can still see the twitching features, the forced smile, the pleading expression as when they peered at me through the bars of their cell in the grim Tombs Prison, New York City.

It was my job, as a police or crime reporter, to attend the day's trial in court, then later to obtain an interview—there was no *sub judice* in New York State—in the cell. This was ordinary routine work. I was, no doubt, an imaginative youth, with a sensitive mind. I grew to know the accused man quite well; as a rule he talked freely; and inevitably, even apart from the evidence produced in court, I caught myself forming an instinctive judgment as to his guilt or innocence.

Pity and horror, accordingly, made an incisive picture in my mind, infinitely more distressing when the man, or woman, had been convicted and was on the way to Sing Sing Prison up-state where electrocution was to take place. Fortunately for me, the paper kept a special man at Sing Sing for the final scene, and I was spared that. I recall, however, the dread all felt of the electric chair; hanging or shooting was child's play compared to this unknown thing. I remember trying in vain to bring comfort by explaining what I had been told, *viz.* that the electric current brought the end before the slower nerve message arrived with the pain.

Another instance of haunting faces survives, before we say goodbye to horror and its effect on memory. I was with the *New York Times* when it occurred and the Health Department tipped us off about a raid at dawn next day on a Mental Home at Amityville, Long Island, conducted by a quack, a place where innocent and sane individuals were secluded by their relatives who wanted them out of the way. It was to be a scoop; but I found every newspaper had sent a man to report it.

The police broke in at dawn and brought out the alleged medical staff with a procession of patients, some of whom, after long incarceration, had actually become insane. The faces of certain of those wretched people I can see vividly today. Sane when they went in, they came out hopelessly insane. I was deeply, horribly impressed.

But beauty etches in memories just as deeply as horror does, and so the Isle of Capri, radiant with its colour and sunshine, flashes up hauntingly, unforgettably, chiefly, I think, because of two vivid personalities associated with it.

For at one end of the island was Gracie Fields, generous-hearted, gracious, sometimes singing among the rocks of her little bay; and at the other far end, in Ana-Capri, behind the high wall of his Torre Matterita, yet accessible to friends who dared his guardian Alsatians, was Axel Munthe, his famous San Michele then almost a museum, but his other villa, a Saracen ruin, rebuilt. We listened to stories and experiences omitted from the well-known book, while we ate slippery spaghetti and drank his Capri wine.

Wandering through rooms crowded with treasures, he pointed to a large table covered with books, challenging me as I picked up one after another in languages I could not name—all translations of the book, dozens of them. These two people, like pins fastening a map on the wall of memory's chamber, present ineffaceable pictures . . . whereas a journey through the Caucasus, for all the legendary wonder of those quite fabulous mountains, with their flowers, their alarming scale of grandeur, the mystery of countless tribes (some of whom still worship trees with bread and salt), their magical dawns and sunsets, yet somehow leave a vague, ill-defined memory—because the element of human personality is left out.

It's rather a jump, I suppose, to watching our milk-fed horse, Azote, running in the Derby, coming in last but one, while the bookies shouted derisively "Milk-o!" An undying memory none the less.

The tale is too long for detail. Briefly, then, in my New York days I knew the secretary to Cornelius Vanderbilt of that distant day. As the Vanderbilt field of interest lay in railways only, never adventuring into patents or invention, this man was free to deal with inventors. He picked out three busy on research into things the world must always need: fuel, clothing, food; and he selected a Westchester county farmer trying to dry milk—a problem of long standing—who suddenly solved it.

Milk, as you know, is the one complete food all females secrete for their young. A glass of milk is seven parts water, the rest the essential solids. This farmer, after years of experiments, suddenly discovered the right method. My friend made a life contract with him and came to London . . . but the doctors questioned whether the great heat employed in the process might not have damaged the salts in the milk, thus preventing good bones . . . so my friend bought a racehorse—of no valuable pedigree—fed it at Epsom for two years on dried milk (nitrogenous food, that is, for the first time) and ran it in the Derby. Its skeleton, poor creature, showing perfectly formed bones, ended in a Paris scientific museum—the case was proved. And so this Derby—my first and only Derby—has left this undying memory.[1]

A ridiculous memory to retain, I agree; it's the excitement and emotion associated with it that keeps it so vividly alive. Dried milk today may be a commonplace, but in 1905-6, or thereabouts, it was a startling novelty.

Then, just when we had turned the corner and money was beginning to pour in, I recall with great vividness my decision, after a week's reflection, to escape from this threat of riches, and start writing for a bare living, but with my liberty, and so went to live in a cheap Pension in the Swiss Jura mountains.

And so, a bit later, stumbled across another memory that crops up with its everlasting life—climbing on the Mont Salève, behind Geneva, with a friend, Ella Maillart, who made the journey across Asia to Pekin with Peter Fleming, a girl of amazing courage and resource, as her *Turkestan Solo* and his *News from Tartary* describe.

To this recovery of memories that cling, as I look back this Christmas, there is no end. And you've had enough, I'm sure. Experiences in Canada, running a disastrous hotel, running also a milk business in Toronto with a herd of Jersey cattle, earning a precarious living in New York as a model to artists, making eau-de-Cologne soap in a back street off Broadway, a mad adventure going to the Rainy River (Minnesota) goldfields, teaching the violin, even French and German, life in the Canadian backwoods for a period . . . all too numerous to make interesting in a few words.

Behind all these more or less trivial experiences, however, there ran the deep steady current of my main interest. This, for some reason, never failed. It is perhaps summed up in a single word: otherworldly. In my autobiography *Episodes Before Thirty*, I described something of these *external* happenings, for I regarded them as such: episodes not of vital, essential importance. Whether starving or homeless, able to pay my way or obliged to sleep in Central Park, despairing or hopefully, this "otherworldly" point of view about it all never once left me.

For my deep interest, ever since boyhood, has lain in the possibility that unusual powers are latent in the human being. States of abnormal consciousness in which these may emerge are the basis of most of my books and stories. While remaining sceptical, I try to keep open minded.

The evidence for certain unusual powers is impressive, and only those familiar with its striking accumulation are worth listening to. Evidence of them crops up in many directions: in mental homes, in séance rooms, yes, in lunatic asylums, as well as in normal life. In genius and its manifestations, in the tale of prodigies, so-called. The field is immense; I have read about and watched such abnormal experiences throughout the years. My books and stories have mostly been speculative and imaginative adventures into this somewhat dangerous region.

I am called the "ghost man"; editors want "ghost stories" from me. Yet my chief interest I should describe as an interest in the Extension of Human Faculty: in other words, latent powers that suggest we are all potentially much greater and more wonderful than we suspect.

The phenomena of the séance room, if not always, must, I feel, be accepted by anyone of really open mind. It is their interpretation that is important. The mental phenomena offer an alternative explanation in what's called "extended telepathy"—telepathy I myself regard as proved—but the so-called "physical phenomena" certainly present puzzling difficulties by no means solved. Indeed the only advance here seems to be—in recent years—the strange fact that the temperature falls while they are in progress, even to the point of fourteen degrees Fahrenheit. The *Scientific American* tests of some years ago seemed to establish this. And there is that unexplained "cold spot" in the tale of Borley Rectory to add its quote by way of evidence. Does this, perhaps, suggest that the energy used is heat?

In any case, it is this deep interest in the possibility of new, latent powers in all of us that has remained my deepest interest through the long years that lie behind me this Christmas. I remain unrepentant in my firm belief that such powers do exist.

And in this connection, a possible advance has just been signalled by Professor Rhine in his *Reach of the Mind* (1947), where he makes out an interesting case for the existence of an extraordinary power in certain minds—the power of influencing objects. His experiments dealt with falling dice tumbling helter-skelter down a chute. A proportion of people, much above the element of chance, influenced the dice to fall as they wished or willed. This power of the mind, if it exists, exists out of our ordinary Time and Space. In different Time, certainly; hence also in different Space, since Time is a function of spatial change and physical movement in Space requires Time.

Now here, of course, we enter a violently controversial region; I most certainly decline to stick my neck out, as the phrase goes, and claim exclusive or positive knowledge. I do, however, believe that, as human beings, we hold latent unusual powers which only manifest, alas, on occasion, sporadically. And these unusual powers include, not merely telepathy and extended telepathy (so as to include a racial, even planetary, memory) but the power to influence objects, even moving objects (as in Professor Rhine's experiments) the recovery of the past and the accessibility of the future, the power to travel and see veridically what's going on in distant places, being buried with suspended animation, the production of internal body heat (sitting naked below zero in comfort)—and the entry, briefly, into conditions of space and time that lie outside our usual dimensions.

The list is too long for a popular sketch like this, but the evidence of such powers lying latent in Smith, Jones and Robinson, is too vast and convincing for any *open-minded* student to cast aside as worthless.

Now, belief is a strange business, you'll agree. It is hard to come by if you're honest with yourself. Each man for himself! I find myself, for instance, believing in the cosmic rays on the reports of others. They pour down on our planet in a devastating flood, terrific, uncontrollable, their origin, their effect upon ourselves, all unknown. Their penetrating power is alarming to my limited understanding. We accept—and believe in—numerous other dicta of science, because, at any rate, we are not qualified to contradict them. They seem valid because they can be reproduced, whereas unusual phenomena due to abnormal consciousness elude this easy but not convincing final test.

So these unusual powers we've talked about seem to boil down to a question of escaping from our normal, everyday consciousness—into some rare condition where our ordinary conceptions of space and time do not hold. Into this immense and speculative field, we cannot plunge now . . . and one difficulty is that anyone who has had strange experiences in this amazing region cannot communicate them to you and me—since language can only express the experience of the race; and any such experiences lie beyond our words. Had any such experience ever come to me personally, I would never take the risk of trying to communicate it, either in speech or writing.

The intelligent reader will understand.

1948.

Note

[1] The "friend", was James R. Hatmaker (1866-1930) who was bequeathed a significant sum in the will of Cornelius Vanderbilt who died in September 1899. This allowed Hatmaker to develop the process necessary to produce the dried milk and he established a London office in November 1903. Blackwood became the managing director in March 1904 and remained so until the success of *John Silence* (1908) allowed him to write full time. Azote ran in several races, mostly in France where Hatmaker had settled. Its one Derby race was in May 1908.

I Speak for Myself

Here I am, in my eighty-first year—a "writer"! An established writer. Not a novelist. Oh, no, a novelist never. Nor with any ambition to become a novelist. The idea to become a writer never once entered my head. Yet here, at this considerable age, I find myself now a "writer"—well, a writer of stories.

So how did this strange result come about? I look back over these eighty years. How did I ever, without any desire or yearning in that direction, become what we call a "writer"? And the answer, I now think, was because I belonged instinctively, without realising it, yes, to that oldest of all fraternities: a story teller. It is, apparently, the most ancient of all arts—if you like to call it such—of Telling a Story. I had, it seemed, a flair. I always enjoyed listening to—and telling—a story. Yet I never guessed this gift, a minor one, I think, lay in me.

Now telling a story doesn't mean inventing a tale out of nothing. It is not necessarily creating. It means, I think, drawing upon some fund of actual experience and adventure, which provide the raw material of what we call a story. A real story has a beginning, middle and end. Good. But life, while supplying the first of these conditions, rarely provides the end—what we call the climax. And there, possibly, pops in the real story-teller's gift: he develops that sequence of some actual experience. Then he invents—creates if you will—that end or climax which transforms the whole into a genuine "story".

11

Thus, in the first place, he must have real experiences to draw upon as his raw material. In my own case, since I am asked to "Speak for Myself", I had an ample supply by the time, quite late in life, I began.

My "ample supply" should be stated. It consisted in what a rolling stone manages to accumulate. Dairy farming in Ontario, then a small hotel in Toronto, then a few months in the backwoods and then, of course, New York—because all these things had failed, you see. In New York I taught French and gave violin lessons. The two friends who found themselves similarly derelict helped out. The verminous, cheap boarding-house, where we had a single filthy room between us, was always behind with the rent. Then, by luck, I got a job as a reporter on *The Evening Sun* at $15 a week. It was, indeed, a half-starved, derelict existence. Time passed. I got a job on the *New York Times* and did well enough. Then the Rainy River Goldfields caught me. With a pass I got to Duluth in Minnesota. Gold, yes. But machinery needed, and capital. A fairy-tale adventure, but a failure again. So back, eventually, to New York. Here an income possible by posing to artists at $3 a sitting; a venture with a canny Scot who, without my knowing it, had stolen the recipe for the Johann Maria eau-de-Cologne—and I got out in time.

All this time, however, abnormal sensitiveness to Beauty—music, sunsets, flowers—whatever it was, had struck and sunk deep.

I had to earn my living. Of course, but my real inner dream was always to find out what the Universe meant, why I was here, what I was aiming at. I read voraciously, using the Public Libraries, also picking up anything I could find about the Subconscious. But it was the Eastern philosophy which appealed to me enormously—my books were the *Upanishads*, Patanjali's *Yoga Aphorisms*, the *Bhagavad Gita*, without which I think I should have gone under. Why my mind took this direction I cannot know; possibly it was a reaction against the narrow evangelical teaching of my childhood. It was, anyhow, an overmastering obsession.

Also, I felt somehow that all the messages of beauty that poured in upon my sensitive make-up, struck my inmost self like a spear, then vanished, yet were not lost. They lay collected, deeply hidden, in the deepest being—one day to emerge.

It is these forgotten messages, I came to think, that much later in life *did* emerge—and in the form of stories, The Subconscious, we are told, never forgets; at the same time it dramatizes its contents. May be! Thus, years later in London, busy with the traffic in Dried Milk, at the time aged thirty-six, these stories, wholly foreign to my daily occupation, boiled up in me—and boiled over in the form of immature stories. I wrote them down. I became a story-teller.

My cupboard was filled with them. I would rather get home to scribble at them than go to plays, dances, theatres, what you will. No editor saw them till, by the merest chance, a friend took home a number of them and sent them to a publisher. So, briefly, after that, I became a story-teller, for better or for worse, in print—and now, years later, find myself called "a writer". Yet it was not a dream fulfilled—to be a novelist never entered my head, nor have I ever attempted a love story; nor, I must confess, have I found the smallest satisfaction on "seeing myself in print" and being called "a writer". But to write stories, trying to give expression to some wild dream, if you will, is rare good fun, also a relief, a safety-valve . . .

I now think that "horror stories" with which I began were little more than the inner drive to express and get rid of—get off my chest, as we say—the accumulated horror

13

of my experiences as a newspaper reporter in New York, when my daily routine was reporting vice, violence, fraud, all the abominations of degraded human types, in my daily work.

Be this as it may, as I look back over so many decades, if I could now live my life again, I know positively what I would choose: namely, to be about twenty-five, with enough to live on so that I need not spend all my time and energy in providing a roof, food, clothing and the like, but to learn the necessary languages, and then to come out East and search, search, search, I mean *search* for a Teacher. I am convinced, in other words, that in the East lies the possibility of learning the real meaning of Life, of Death, of the Universe . . . for I am now more convinced than ever that the Eastern wisdom, though hard to find, offers the true solution to these deep problems that trouble all thinking minds today as always.

3 December 1949.

How I Became Interested in Ghosts

As some of you may know, I have a rather strong liking for Queer Stories—Ghost Stories. I prefer the term Queer Stories, ones that have no explanation at all, whereas Ghost Stories have several explanations. I was thinking the other day when all this first started in me. It dates back to my early childhood. There's no doubt that the man who fostered it in me, perhaps only woke what was in the blood, and that was my own father, who liked ghost stories too. He loved queer stories and used to tell them awfully well. The one drawback to them sometimes was that they had a moral. I like the story without a moral. He wouldn't have anything to do with spirits. He was very religious, very strictly religious in certain ways and wanted to warn me off that dangerous country. So this is the story—this is how it began.

There was a poor fellow who suffered from epileptic fits. They were very serious fits; they came at intervals and none of the doctors had been able to help him. He'd been to them all. Then one day a friend of his said, "Now, look here, these doctors aren't helping at all. Why don't you ask the spirits?" Well the man didn't know what he was talking about and said, "What do you mean, ask the spirits?" "Well," his friend said, "some people, they get advice from spirits." And the man said, "Oh, do they. I didn't know that. I hadn't heard of that sort of thing." "Well, it isn't very easy to get hold of," said his friend, "but I think I could arrange it for you, and we'll see what happens."

Well, the epileptic, who was at the end of his tether with regard to being cured by doctors—I think the treatment in those days wasn't as effective as it is now—couldn't put it off. He listened to his friend who said, rather tongue-in-cheek perhaps, "I'll choose a soothsayer and you go to him and hear what he has to say."

Well, in due course that happened. The epileptic went, stated his case and asked for help, and help was eventually offered—but in such a strange way that the sufferer still kept his tongue in his cheek, thinking what the Americans call, "baloney". He was told to do this. They gave him a little locket, not a valuable one, but a little silver one, I think it was, and they said: "Our advice is to tell you to wear this round your neck, day and night. Always wear it next to the skin—and on the heart side of the body, if you can. But don't open it. You must never open it."

They told him this, and he went away. He was a very sincere sort of fellow and having given his word and his promise, he stuck to it, and for the next week he wore this troublesome thing, until he got used to it. He didn't care for gadgets and mascots and things. He wore it round his neck—day and night. This went on for some weeks, to his great surprise, because a fit was due by now. But a fit didn't come. The fits stopped. It ran from weeks to months. No sign of a fit. He dared to consider himself really cured, though he still wore it round his neck and never opened it, though he had great curiosity towards it. Friends laughed at it, friends who saw it when he was bathing—this silly mascot round his neck. Then one day, certainly a couple of years later—I can't remember dates—the curiosity was too great. He opened this little thing, a tuppeny-ha'penny locket, which he'd been carrying about for so long, and inside he saw there was some writing. It was extremely small—you could hardly read it without a magnifying glass. But he managed to decipher it, and it said:

Let him alone till he drop into hell.

"Oh," said my sister, who was listening to the story as well, "they did leave him alone father, didn't they."

My father just nodded.

That was the kind of story he would tell us. Not an eye-opener, but from that moment—I think I must have been about sixteen then—I had an intense desire to tell these ghost stories and see a ghost for myself. That was the way my hobby started, and I tried to see ghosts when I could. And the only way I could do that, I decided, was to sleep in haunted houses and wait till the ghost came. My father had no objections, and he was very helpful because he was able to tell me certain badly haunted houses that were going to be investigated by the Society for Psychical Research—that was, if they were worth investigating. This was first class, as it saved me all the trouble of going about hunting and listening to absurd stories.

The first house of that kind that was so badly haunted that people were leaving was in a little side street in Knightsbridge—one of those little streets that run down from Knightsbridge to Montpelier Square. It was what we used to call a cheap little boarding house. It was a very nice, neat little place, and it was kept by a Mrs. Garnier. Her husband was the butler and she had saved a little and put it into this house. All her guests, from time to time, saw this ghost. I went to the trouble—and it was considerable trouble—to look them up and question them as to what they'd seen and under what conditions. It was very interesting to me. Mrs. Garnier herself, a nice little old woman, rather talkative, she'd seen it, and said she couldn't live in this house any longer. I'll tell you her story later, but I'll tell you one of the others first.

On the top floor were two bank clerks, Scotsmen. They both worked for the same bank. I looked them up and they told me a very extraordinary story, and there was no question of it, you couldn't doubt their word. They'd both seen this thing and described what happened.

It was a small room, because a partition had been put up, which made a tiny extra room, which was the landlady's bedroom. No door in it—just a thin partition. It just cut off enough of their room to make the space for a bed, and that's where she slept and that's where, as I'll tell you later, she had her experience, and a very unpleasant one it was.

The figure seen by all these people—and they all agreed on it—was a woman. Not alarming you'd think, but a tall, thin woman with marks of suffering and pain on her face, and very sad looking indeed. The brothers had two separate beds, one in the corner under the little window and the other on the other side, by the door, where the younger one slept. And the younger one told me this.

"Some nights I've been greatly disturbed by my brother walking in his sleep. Of course, we had no light on at night, we just slept. And I'd tell him, go back to bed. But he never obeyed—he didn't seem to hear. Occasionally he'd pass between me and the very small window and I could see the outline. Well, Tom (as I'll call him) was one of those fellows who preferred the long night shirts. He didn't wear pyjamas, and when he flitted past the window you could see the outline of a long, draped figure. But you couldn't see distinctly, you couldn't see the face, just the bare outline. My brother had always denied sleepwalking but then, of course, he wouldn't know, would he? On this particular night the figure passed across the little window and, by George, it wasn't Tom. It was a woman. I would swear it was a woman. And it disappears, like a shadow against the partition, which was just by my bed. And then, I can't swear to this because there wasn't enough light, but that figure seemed to me to ooze into that partition, to melt into it if you like, and at the same moment my brother, who was wide awake all the time, shouted 'I can't see it', and at that moment there was a scream of terror that was very terrible—the old lady had seen something. And I heard her voice, which was very shaken with terror, shout 'In the name of the Holy Trinity what's troubling you?', and then there was a crash and silence."

Well, the two brothers were out on that landing in a moment. Her door wasn't locked and they burst their way in. In the light—she had a candle—she was there on the bed, white with terror, speechless. She later told me her story.

"I'd been lying there with the light on, trying to get to sleep, when suddenly I saw something coming through this partition. It came right through into the room. And it was the woman—the woman I'd seen before in the house—a tall, thin woman with suffering, sad, melancholy face, and when I said those words, 'In the name of the Holy Trinity what's troubling you?', this dreadful figure raised a hand across her throat and I could just see that there was a dark mark across her throat. The next second she was gone, and I heard the gentlemen coming in to help."

That was her story. They did what they could, of course. They had to believe her. Her reason was solid. There was something that slipped through that partition and showed itself to the person on the other side.

Well, I felt very hopeful and thought that I'm going to see this. I spoke to the other people across the hall. They'd all seen this figure—the same figure, though they described it differently, but they all described the mark across her throat, the sadness in her face, and a tall, lean woman. Mrs. Garnier had either a niece or a daughter, I've forgotten which, who was a girl of about eighteen, and she was playing a minor part in *Dorothy*. You may not remember it, it was long ago, *Dorothy* by Hayden Coffin. It was a light musical play which had great success—it was the rage of London at the time.[1] Well, this girl—I can't remember her name—used to come home at 1.00 in the morning—the last bus I suppose—and go into the house and into the hall. There, on the table in the hall, was always a glass of milk and something to eat. Well, this girl didn't believe in all this. She thought they'd made it all up. It made no impression on her at all. She took her glass of milk and began to drink and then saw this woman pacing across the table, quite close to her, a grim face of sorrow and pain. She dropped her glass—smashed to bits, spilling the milk.

I thought that I'd got enough evidence of this house now and that I ought to spend a night in it, but before I did, I went to see the cemetery inspector of the region. Someone had told me that if I saw him, he'd tell me the story of this woman, which would give the whole thing more point. He told me that about fifty years ago an elderly lady lived there, a rather mysterious person, and she'd been found in bed, strangled, and there was a lot of money under the mattress. I don't know if it was murder or if she'd done it herself. I mention it because it adds weight to the story for the Society for Psychical Research. So I arranged a night there. Mrs. Garnier would be out. The Scottish brothers would be at their bank. The girl wasn't there any more and the house was empty. They gave me a key. I took some food. I went upstairs. I meant to sit on the ground floor. It was a June night, as hot as blazes. I was awfully keen, awfully interested, and thought I was going to see something. I didn't take a book. I was learning shorthand and had a copy of the *Pall Mall Gazette*, and I was writing this shorthand over the Leader. It kept my mind concentrated and didn't excite, you see. I thought that was a rather good idea.

The street got quieter and quieter. The pub closed—I don't know what time that was—and a few people came out shouting and singing. It got very still indeed. There was the traffic—an occasional hansom went past, an occasional policeman spoke, but there was not a sound otherwise. Very hot—but in spite of the heat, I began to feel very cold. I was aware of being cold—and I was cold *inside*. I'd read that the heat is the energy used to produce these appearances and that got on my mind, you know. That's the first time I felt frightened.

Well, I got on with my shorthand and then I heard a noise downstairs. Now, of course, in a haunted house, if you hear a noise, you must go and investigate at once. Well, I didn't want to. But I forced myself to get up and I went down the stairs. Luckily I had left the gas lights on. I went right down to the kitchen, but not a sign of anything and I came back. There I sat for another two, three hours, waiting and waiting. And I thought, what happens if that woman comes up and into this room. I began, in a certain way, to hope she wouldn't come. And then came that emotion that I was so keen to see something that I thought, I hope she will.

At two in the morning, I turned the gas out and went upstairs, one flight, and made up my mind to sleep in the room where the two Scots brothers had seen their vision. How I wished they were with me, someone to talk to and compare notes with. Someone as comfort; yes, that's the truth. I don't know why you feel horror about a ghost, but you do. I went upstairs, taking a lit candle, even though I had the gas light. I gave a little shudder as I opened the door into the room and something shot from under the bed and out of the window. For a moment it gave me a little jump—it showed what state of nerves I was in. But I had control and told myself if anything comes, I'll be ready for it. Then I slept down on the bed where the elder brother had seen the old lady melt through the partition. And, for all I know, that old house is still there now, and those things may still be going on.[2]

13 October 1951.

Notes

[1] Blackwood implies he was sixteen when he undertook this investigation, i.e. after March 1885, but that is unlikely and in any case contradicted by his reference to the musical *Dorothy* being all the rage. This did not start its London run until the end of September 1886, but its popularity rose when it shifted to the Prince of Wales Theatre in December 1886. It ran until April 1889. Blackwood refers to it being a hot June evening. He was in Switzerland until the end of June 1887 and the play had ceased by June 1889, so he must have undertaken this investigation in June 1888, when he was nineteen. However, the weather was unseasonably cold until the end of June 1888, so either Blackwood has misremembered the month or the weather was not as hot as he recalled.

[2] I have been unable to find the exact address of this house. Although there is a Mrs. Garnier living in London at that time, it is not close enough to where Blackwood suggests and neither does her husband fit the description. Blackwood implies the house was between Knightsbridge and Montpelier Square. Edmund Gurney, one of the

leading authorities in the Society for Psychical Research lived at 26 Montpelier Square and may well have alerted Blackwood to the house. However, Gurney died in Brighton on 23 June 1888, and it is unlikely Blackwood would have been allowed to investigate the house on his own at that time.

The Midnight Hour

In the distant days when I was so eager to *see* a ghost with my own eyes, I recall a singular example of the strange effects of terror; and I don't mean the terror of meeting a tiger, or a burglar face to face with a pistol raised; I mean spiritual or ghostly terror, whichever you prefer.

I've always felt a psychological interest in these alleged effects of terror: paralysis of movement, speechlessness, hair turning white (apparently quite unsubstantiated) and the rest. With regard to the latter, you may know the delightful tale of the old lady who was so terrified by a ghost that her wig, carefully draped on the dressing-table, was white next morning.

But coming back to my own personal experiences, I once came across a result of terror that was quite new to me. If you don't want to hear about it, just turn over the page to the enchanting pictures you will find. If you care to listen, however, may I add, before my little tale, that it was only years later that I came across a reference to this particular effect of ghostly terror in Kipling. It is the only reference I know. Kipling, you must admit, was a prince of accurate observations. He mentions it. All right. If you're still reading, here's what happened.

Eager to see a ghost with my own eyes I was lucky enough to get advance notice of haunted houses the Psychical Research Society considered worth investigating; cases, that is, with good evidence behind them. Among these was a certain unfurnished house in a Brighton Square. The story was horrible. A man-servant in the household, crazily in love with a housemaid, had crashed the girl over the banisters to her death. The evidence of the crime, as also the evidence supporting its alleged re-enactment in ghostly forms, was overwhelming.

Rather by subterfuge, I got the keys of the empty house from the Brighton agents, and I well recall the agent's admission, when I pressed him, that the house was said to be haunted. That admission (from a house agent) took some getting, but I got it. And I planned to spend a night in this unfurnished, empty haunted house.

I had arranged to take a sister with me, but at the last moment she got "cold feet". She just couldn't face it. Nor did I blame her. In the daylight of the sunny Brighton front it was easy; when the dusk fell and shadows began to creep, it was different. It so happened that our hostess exclaimed suddenly, "Oh, I'll come if you want a companion. I don't believe in this ghostly stuff and, anyhow, I don't care a damn!"[1]

We went together. It was about 11.30 p.m. The night was still. No wind. And the sound of the surf fell booming through the deserted square as we made our quiet way, not talking much, I noticed. A moon, almost at the full, silvered the empty square and silent streets. Everybody seemed in bed. My companion, my hostess, whom I knew slightly, was a youngish woman, gay, cheery, chatty. But as we entered the square and approached the house, her chatty volubility, I noticed, died away. It was all so silent, so deserted. The bright moonlight, the booming of the surf, these alone struck our senses. We padded on together then in silence towards the empty house. I recall wishing I had been alone. I didn't quite like her increasing silence.

And then we reached the house in the corner of the square. It looked menacing to me in that blaze of moonlight.

I had brought with me a thermos, candles, matches, food and a rug. First making sure there was no one in sight, above all a wandering bobby, we mounted the steps and I put the key in. Once inside, I closed the front door behind me and took out my matchbox. For this was before the days of electric torches, I must mention. And as I opened the box, there was a sound of someone coughing close beside me. There, standing in the darkness of the entrance hall, someone coughed. It was a man's cough, I swear.

It gave me a nasty turn, I admit. There was someone else in the empty house besides our two selves. There was no possible doubt in my mind about that cough. It was close beside me as I stood in that darkened hall. It was a natural, not a premeditated cough. A shiver ran up my back. Yet, that strange thing, as later interrogation proved, was that my companion had *not* heard it. It came to my ears only. Now, please remember that of seeing a ghost I had no faintest fear. I was bursting to see one. I had no fear of that kind, for my interest was far stronger than any superstitious terror. But that cough, close against my ears in the darkness—well it gave me a nasty turn as I've said. And, to make things worse, I had opened my matchbox upside down, so that its contents scattered on to the stone floor—and had to be picked up. A rat, a mouse even, anything might start a fire. Laboriously, while my friend said nothing, I picked them up and lit my candle.

So, here and now, was the immediate problem. Somebody else besides ourselves was in this empty, unfurnished house. They might be crooks, using a haunted house as their hiding place. A dozen explanations flashed through my mind. But, at any rate, we must first search the house from floor to ceiling.

Persuading my companion with some difficulty that this was first necessary, we carried it out faithfully, from the kitchen and scullery to the servants' rooms on the top floor. A nasty, creepy business, I admit it was, expecting any minute to see a face in the shadows or a figure slinking round a door. I think the servants' attics were the worst. It was here, of course, the murderer had found his victim before he crashed her over the banisters to her death. We found—we saw—nothing and eventually we sat up to wait for events in a small room at the top of the stairs leading from the attics to the lower floors. We sat on the bare boards, a lit candle shining through the door of a half-open cupboard . . . waiting, waiting, waiting, and listening, listening, listening. We spoke little and, for some reason, in whispers only. The moonlight fell in slantingly across the floor. We just heard the distant booming of the surf at the end of the square. Otherwise there was silence, silence broken only by our rare whispered remarks.

I was expectant, keyed up, hopefully, I admit it. But I had no sense of fear. If, by any lucky chance, as the hours wore on, there came a voice, step, or some evidence of anybody moving, I was ready on the instant, to jump up and investigate. I *might*, God knows, see the terrified housemaid in full flight down the stairs. I *might* see the love-crazed man full tilt at her heels, hunting her down to her terrible death. I *might*, with any luck, see a ghost at last!

For my companion, so eagerly did I sit there waiting as the hours passed, I admit I had little thought; and then—suddenly—it struck me: "Does she feel the same? Is she perhaps a bit scared? Could she jump up and come with me?" I think her prolonged silence made me suddenly ask these questions. And I imagine an unwelcome doubt about her state of mind caused them.

We were sitting, as I said, side by side on the bare boards of the little room at the top of the stairs. The candlelight through the opened door of the cupboard made her face plainly visible. I glanced down at her sideways.

"If I hear a step or a voice," I whispered, "we ought to go out and investigate it at once. Are you all right?"

But the sight of her face froze me stiff. She did not answer. Her face, not uncomely, had somehow gone back to the face of childhood. It was the face of a girl, lines and wrinkles all ironed out. It was a face masked by utter terror, its youthfulness somehow terrible.

My own reactions were immediate. I must get her out of the house. My mind worked quickly at that moment. If a step or a voice had come outside on the stairs or landing, she could not have moved for terror. I realised that. Her terror had been growing, increasing for hours evidently, but I had not noticed it. Had anything "ghostly" intervened just then, she would simply have passed out. I knew it. I felt sure of it. I must get her out of the house at once. To be caught in an empty house with an unconscious young woman on my hands at 2 a.m., with police and press inquisitive publicity and the rest, would have been an unenviable situation.

And so it was. Explaining as convincingly as I could that nothing was now likely to happen—it was almost early morning and we had sat waiting for hours—I took her arm and we crawled together, side by side, down the long stairs and so out into the street and the fresh keen air blowing from the sea. And she told me frankly that for hours she had been too scared to move or speak, not even whisper.

And, as I mentioned, it was only years later that I came across a ghost story of Kipling's where he mentions this strange effect of real terror that blots out the adult face and masks it with the innocence of childhood.[2] My experience at least can claim this backing from a close observer. An unusual thrill had certainly come my way though it was not, after all, the thrill I had hoped for, the thrill of seeing a ghost at last.

24 November 1948.

Note

[1] In a letter written years later to an unidentified fan of his works Blackwood revealed that the lady who accompanied him was " . . . a misguided but charming lady who had persuaded herself I should make a good husband, though such a thought had never even entered my head". The house was in Hove rather than Brighton.

[2] I believe the story Blackwood is alluding to is "At the End of the Passage" (1890) where, at one point, Kipling writes:

> As a sponge rubs a slate clean, so some power unknown to Spurstow had wiped out of Hummil's face all that stamped it for the face of a man, and he stood at the doorway in the expression of his lost innocence. He had slept back into terrified childhood.

Minor Memories

I've often wondered why insignificant memories cling so vividly, so tenaciously, when the incidents we thought so important fade after a few years, lose their sharp edges . . . die.

Possibly, it occurs to me, one reason is that these insignificant, minor memories stick because they were associated with an *unusual* emotion, or, at least, a novel emotion. For these insignificant incidents go on shouting along memory's corridors like a broken disc, repeating themselves endlessly.

Now, I think childhood memories are boring, but this one I'd like to mention for, when just old enough to grip the lower bar of the nursery window, I saw the face of deity. Yes, I saw God. My evangelical family spoke much of God, but I had no idea what he looked like. On this occasion I saw Him face-to-face. I was puzzled by the webbing about the awful visage, also by something that hung below where the shoulders should have begun. Naturally, it was a balloon from the Crystal Palace sailing over Kent. An indelible memory.

Then up swims another face that refuses to fade after some sixty years—the face of D. L. Moody, the Revivalist. With Sankey, his hymn-singing colleague, he often stayed in my father's house. With my father's sincere evangelical conviction, they were welcome, and the question "Are you saved?" pervaded the atmosphere, and I was terrified lest Moody, sooner or later, would corner me and ask that dreadful question. For I didn't really know. I avoided him with the cunning of a Red Indian, hiding behind furniture or curtains when I sensed his near approach. C. T. Studd, the cricketer, and Lord Radstock, also vehement evangelists, were often in the house, but I had no fear of them.[1] But Moody, with his crisp black beard, his squat figure, his powerful personality, above all his hypnotic eyes . . . Moody frightened me. Luckily he never cornered me, assuming no doubt that, as a son of the house, I *was* "saved".

It's a story he told at the dinner table that fixes this trivial memory. One evening in Liverpool, on his way to a meeting, an uncontrollable instinct came to him to cross the road. He did so—fairly shot across. Years later at one of his enthusiastic meetings, a sinner stood up to announce that he was "saved". He went on to confess his sins, among which was a hatred of Moody so intense that he decided to kill him. He followed him down the street, his knife ready in his hand to strike when, suddenly, Moody, without rhyme or reason, shot across the road. Years later, as a *New York Times* correspondent, I visited him in Northfield, Massachusetts, to see his great work with schools and hospitals and, all fear gone, I asked him to confirm this incident. He did so.

Another undying, but trivial, memory concerns a man who looked me in the eye and convinced me he was a murderer. I felt what he said to me in that moment gave himself away. I have no proof—no proof exists. The little incident happened fifty years ago, yet I see his face today as vividly as I see Moody's face. I could draw the features faithfully. As a New York newspaper man I had known murderers by the dozen, but all have faded away. Not this man's. Briefly it was like this.

31

I was one of a moose-hunting party in Northern Ontario, my hosts a Professor of Semitic Languages and his huntress wife.[2] Starting from Montreal we left the Canadian Pacific Railway at Mattawa, a wayside halt on the edge of the wild moose country. We went by canoe to Cogawanna Lake as our headquarters.[3] Each of us had a backwoods guide and canoe. Separating in various directions for several days at a stretch, we met again at our camp and compared notes.

Now, on our train from Montreal, was another moose-hunter's party from New York, like ourselves and, as moose cover great distances, we feared they might disturb our particular hunting region. Their camp, though, was well away from ours.

The evening before we were to leave for civilisation something unusual happened. It was towards sunset, October, the big lake unruffled, when we saw something gleaming oddly some miles away. No Indians about. What could it be? Glasses solved the puzzle: a man paddling a nine-foot canoe, with a branch! It came slowly nearer as we watched. It was our friend from the train. Odd indeed. Miles from his party's camp.

I remember I sensed trouble ahead. I also remember the way my own Adirondack guide, Hank, somehow naturally took command. His experiences of the backwoods, hunting parties, accidents and the like, was immense. He was also a bit of a philosopher in his rough way. "Let me handle this, folks," he warned us, so we did.

I stood back by my little tent and watched. The canoeist, with his ridiculous branch as paddle, was exhausted, as Hank helped him land. But not too exhausted to talk, though I couldn't catch his words. Hank, I noticed, said nothing; just helped him up to the fire, where our supper was cooking, and made him comfortable. The man went on talking. Slowly, on a sign from Hank, we gathered round, bringing blankets (air frosty) and whiskey, but, taking our cue from Hank, asking no questions. We talked idle commonplaces, while exchanging glasses. Hank controlled the talk with remarkable instinctive tact.

Of course, we wanted to know what had happened. Why this strange arrival? In fact the man was telling us: he never stopped. No matter how often both ourselves and Hank tried to choke him off, nothing could stop him. The impression deepened: he was telling a made-up story. Repeating and repeating. It never varied. He was reciting something he had learned by heart. I wish I could recall the exact dialogue when Hank tried to stop him and switch it off.

Briefly, his story was plausible enough. From their Camp on Garden Lake, fifty miles away, he had set off with his guide, Jake the Swede, to cross to the opposite shore, using a nine-foot canoe. Rough water—they upset. Holding hands across the up-turned craft they hoped the wind would drift them on to a tiny rocky island half way. Within a hundred yards they realised they would just miss it. Jake broke away, saying he'd swim for it. Water icy. His companion just made the island, then collapsed. Never saw Jake again. Next morning found the canoe caught by roots. Hunted for Jake in vain. He cut a branch as paddle and made for our camp, owing to favourable wind.

Now it was only later, on the train home, that we compared notes and agreed there had been violence, possibly a fight. No proof. We took him with us the next morning to the Mattawa train.

What anchors this so tenaciously in my memory is something that happened when we all went to bed. The professor and his wife shared a tent, the three guides slept under a lean-to, my own little tent alone had room for the guest. It was as we undressed in the open air before taking to the blankets that our guest turned to me and said the words I can still hear today: "By the by, if I talk in my sleep, please wake me."

He did not talk in his sleep. Next day, on the way home, Hank and a guide broke away. They found Jake's body in deepish water close to the little island in Garden Lake. A wound on the back of his head might, of course, have been caused by *maskinongé*, the giant and ferocious pike which haunts those lakes. It might also have been due to a struggle over the nine-foot canoe which won't hold two men for ever. I was twenty-three at the time but the man's face as he said, "Wake me if I talk in my sleep", remains as vividly in memory as of yesterday.

And somehow . . . the way the mind works . . . this leads dangerously into a delightful region: IF and IF ONLY.

"Dangerous" because there's no end to it. "IF", "IF ONLY" I hadn't said this or that, done this or that, life could have been otherwise, perhaps nearer to the heart's desire. I won't embark on this dangerous quest, but one item I may be allowed to pick out, in my own case. For here the "IF" is pregnant of a change that must have affected the whole course of life. But for the "IF", I should never have published anything.

So here, briefly, I have the egotistical facts.

In the horrible New York boarding house where, aged twenty-one, I lived in a room with two other half starving friends, there broke in one day, a youngster, Angus Hamilton. He was a step-son of Sir Arthur Wing Pinero, looking for a job, though he had a small income through Daniel Frohman, the theatrical impresario. A good chap, but a bore. He finally got a job on my paper, the New York *Evening Sun*. Having no money to spend we stayed indoors and, to fill the time, I used to tell stories. They came easily and naturally into my head and, well, I just "spouted" them. It seemed I had an endless power of pouring them out. And my audience was thrilled.

Years passed. I came back to London. One day a hansom stopped in Piccadilly and out jumped a young fellow I didn't recognise. It was Angus Hamilton, just off to China as a Reuters correspondent. He came to my Chelsea room for a cup of tea. We talked over old days in New York. He mentioned the wild tales I told in that verminous boarding house—never sent to magazines because I thought them poor. He took away a dozen of these third-rate scripts.

Why I had written these tales . . . ? I can't say. They boiled up in me with such intense desire to express them that my only aim was to give up *any* invitation, theatre or dinner, and get back to my typewriter. This had become my chief, fundamental object for a long time.

Hamilton went off to China and I never saw him again, but a few weeks later a publisher wrote accepting what he called my book of ghost stories. Hamilton had sent them in without telling me. And when in due course *The Empty House* [1906] appeared, it somehow caught the eagle eye of Hilaire Belloc, then literary editor of the *Morning Post*, and Belloc, liking ghost stories, gave it a generous word which persuaded me to try again, at the age of thirty-six.

So here was a big "IF" indeed. *If* I hadn't been in Piccadilly when that hansom passed; *if* Hamilton hadn't crossed my path in New York; *if* Hilaire Belloc hadn't liked ghost stories and spotted my little volume, I don't think I would ever have taken to writing tales for publication . . . and life would have been quite different.

8 September 1949.

Notes

[1] Granville Waldegrave (1833-1913), 3rd Baron Radstock was effectively Blackwood's cousin, via various marriages. Blackwood's mother had been married before to the Duke of Manchester. His sister, Lady Caroline Montagu was the mother of Susan Calcraft (1833-1892) who had married Lord Radstock in 1858. The youngest of his nine children was Mary Waldegrave (1872-1935), with whom Blackwood would play as a child, and she grew up to marry one of Blackwood's closest friends, Edwyn Bevan whom I have speculated was one of the sources of inspiration for John Silence. Susan Calcraft's father, John Hales Calcraft owned the Rempstone estate in Dorset where Edwyn and Mary Bevan later lived and which was the setting for the John Silence story "The Nemesis of Fire".

[2] The Professor of Semitic Languages was John Dyneley Prince (1868-1945) the nephew of Ellin Lowery who had married James Speyer in 1897 when Blackwood was Speyer's Private Secretary. His huntress wife was Adeline Loomis (1868-1944), his step-sister. Blackwood notes he was twenty-three at the time, but that's very unlikely as he did not know Prince until 1897, and this episode probably happened in 1898 when Blackwood was twenty-nine.

[3] Lake Cogawanna is now called Lac Caugnawana in Quebec. The journey from Mattawa is more portage than canoe and, in a straight line, is about twenty-five miles (40 km). This episode became the basis for Blackwood's story "Skeleton Lake".

My Strangest Christmas

Two incidents occur to me, both without any explanation.

The first happened in New York, fifty-three years ago. It concerns a woman's stocking, though I never knew who the woman was. I was in my early twenties, stranded with no job in sight, sharing a room in an East 19th Street boarding-house with two others, equally "on their uppers". It was Christmas Eve; we had just enough for a meal of sorts round the corner, and on our way out a parcel in the hall addressed to me, left by a messenger boy, was an exciting find.

Climbing upstairs again, I opened it. A big silk stocking! A silly joke, no doubt, a stocking to hang up that night. But it was stuffed to the wide brim with tinned meat, biscuits, socks, gloves, etc. etc., and right at the bottom an envelope containing $100. £20! There was no hint of the sender's name. Few persons able to send such a gift knew my address. I speculated endlessly . . . made discreet, tentative enquiries, all without result; to this day I don't know who the sender was.[1]

The second strange incident happened in London many years later—in Christmas week. I had begun scribbling books by then, but the exchequer was wobbly—very. Among the morning letters was a cheap-looking envelope addressed in capital letters by hand; it looked like an advertisement of sorts; indeed, my first instinct was to throw it aside, unopened. Inside was a half sheet of rough paper with "IN PAYMENT OF A DEBT" in ink in capital letters. There was no name, no date, no address, merely this half sheet and—a £50 bank note. The postmark on the envelope was Peckham.

I could think of no one, either here or in Canada and the USA of earlier years, who owed me £50. I thought of advertising in the *Morning Post* by way of discreet enquiry. I told my friends, all without result; the handwriting, of course, betrayed nothing. For some time I felt uncomfortable about using the money, though I hardly know precisely why. In the end I did use it, persuaded by imaginative friends that some reader had liked a book of mine and wished to say "Thank You" anonymously.

24 December 1948.

Note

[1] Blackwood used this incident as the basis for his story "A Suspicious Gift" in *The Empty House* (1906).

The Little People & Co.

Yes, I know it's Xmas time and all that, and at Xmas I like indulging one of my bad habits: I let my imagination out for a run. I think you do the same probably. We needn't believe in Santa Claus and reindeer, but it's a relief to take a deep breath and play about with other forms of imagination. Time makes a kind of halt at Xmas—as it does at the New Year—and there's a sort of space to fill.

Dreaming a bit, fantasy, above all—stories round an open fire.

As an old bachelor, with no children to hop and skip about my knees pleading with fairy eyes for stories, I try to fill that space, if only for my own pleasure: fairies, hobgoblins, trolls, nothing really monstrous or frightening, but certainly—ghosts.

Rossetti, I read somewhere, had what he called his "Imaginative Creed". Well, I've got one myself. And mine is really a beauty. For, you see, it includes a sort of conviction that our old planet has other occupants beside our own rather disappointing Human Race. It's an exciting and interesting conception, at any rate, and quite apart from what evidence there may be for these other-worldly occupants.

And I don't mean merely ghosts. As a boy, I always longed to see a ghost, talk with him, handle him, see him with these two normal organs that sometimes go astray with cataracts. That longing still persists, no doubt, but I have long since come to the conclusion that a ghost is a pedestrian, even vulgar fellow. He has no poetry, no enterprise, no sense of adventure, but just goes on repeating himself; anti-social almost, definitely against progress. Even when he pushes his way into the séance room, he is less intelligent than he was in life. As a rule, at any rate, let's say . . . as a rule . . .

With Witchcraft and Demonology, so-called, it's much the same; I shrink from the gangster ingredient both contain. With mediaeval glamour, again, I find it a bit repulsive, unwholesome and, anyhow, most of it has now been effectively debunked by the explanations of modern psychology, schizophrenia, and the rest—candidates all for the psychiatrist.

And so I come back to the more fragrant idea of children pleading with their fairy eyes for stories. Ah— "fairy", that's the operative word. And for my part, I plump whole-heartedly for the Company they derive from: The Little People. By way of imaginative, tactful politeness, I add "and Co."

Imagination, remember, has no time to deal laboriously with what we call evidence, astonishing and cumulative though it is, for the existence of this delightful tiny race. Ten honest, observant persons who have just seen a rabbit cross the road, will give utterly divergent descriptions of the occurrence. Evidence cuts both ways. Imagination, wisely, pays no attention to it. Yet the number of honest, observant people who have described to me their apprehension— visual, tactful, audible—of having perceived a member of the Little People, lies hidden in my private note-books.

As I look back and watch those "tireless black oxen, treading the years", as Yeats has it, well—I take the leash off my irrepressible Imagination and let it run wild into the park.[1] Now, hadn't I better admit at once, taking my courage in my teeth, that I really think *I believe in their existence?*

40

Were it not for what's called a post bag, I think I would. We humans are not the only beings on the planet. It was born, of course, this belief, in early youth when my father drove me across the Island of Skye to visit his old school-friend, the MacLeod of MacLeod at Dunvegan Castle on the north-west coast, telling me, too, that they kept under a glass case a Fairy Banner stolen from the Fairies; and that I must not laugh or ask questions. But at sixteen I was too thrilled and breathless to do either. The seed of enquiry was sown, doubtless, in fruitful soil; for my young imagination, even at sixteen, was already blazing fiery trails about the planet, and *he* probably thought Fairies were less dangerous than enquiries in Spiritualism, etc.

So much for the start of my interest in the Little People. But the Black Oxen trod on and on. As nobody is listening, now, I can say frankly that my belief took on more substance—after voluminous reading, of course, and listening to others. Sometimes I hardly know how many feet I actually possessed, but two of them at least I kept firmly on the ground. I had collected evidence, so-called, for numerous *sensory* encounters, though I never saw anything myself. It was, really, quite staggering in both matter and—yes, I must admit—convincing evidence. Obviously I have no time to summarise it at the moment. Evidence, anyhow, we agreed is tiresome. Imagination has no truck with it. "Everything possible to be believed," said Blake, "is an image of Truth."

And thus it was that the Black Oxen drew me towards the circle of Yeats—and my dog strained at the leash. Before gifts of that high standard I, naturally, kept quiet. He was interested at the time in a Secret Society, so-called, into which, on his advice, I was eventually admitted as a student.[2] I say "student" because amongst other things it entailed a knowledge of the Hebrew alphabet, whose endless correlations contained a complete system of Hebrew magic. If not an entirely new world to my searching mind, the use of sound and names at least provided material years later for a book, *The Human Chord* [1910], and the search for the mysterious Name of God, kept hidden by leaving out all vowels.

At any rate, I recall vividly my talks with Yeats, and if he never actually confirmed belief in any visual appearance of the Little People, he somehow contrived to increase my belief in the probability of their existence.

And then George Russell hove in sight—"A.E." as the poets know him—and my breathless dog, Imagination, broke the leash and dashed off full speed into the unknown. Naturally, I tore after him. A.E.'s *Candle of Vision* [1918] lay fresh in my mind. I wanted to talk about it, but *he* wanted to talk about a book of mine, *The Centaur* [1911].[3] And a "talk" with A.E. is a miss-statement: *he* talked, I listened. I slid in a question under the counter now and again, but my role was listening. It remains an unforgettable experience. Thus, perhaps, Coleridge talked. It was not merely the flow of language, but the richness of imaginative conception, the coherence of thought and ideas, their faultless presentation. Yeats, when he talked, rapt me into the fairyland of his haunted Celtic Twilight. His voice, half intoning, was so charged with musical cadences it was almost a song: one's critical faculties went to sleep . . . But A.E. set the mind ablaze. That my *Centaur* was his theme doubtless flattered my vanity but, apart from that, his rolling words were a whirlwind, a tornado, that rushed me back into the fabulous grandeur of the Caucasus where Prometheus still lay, defying the Furies and the vulture, and the *Argo* pointed its silver prow towards Colchis. My memories of that region became alive again, the *pretty* valleys of Galway faded out . . .

But I managed to slide under the counter a question of sorts: why, with my interest of years, had I never actually seen one of the Little People? To which his quiet answer was delightful: "Go to Sligo; pass a summer night on the slopes of Ben Bulben; I guarantee you will have an experience of a kind you will never forget!"

Ben Bulben, of course, is that mount beyond Drumcliff where, I think, Yeats now lies buried, which is so haunted by Fairies and the Little People, that it is avoided by the natives.[4] I know it well by name, and some day I must go there and put A.E.'s guarantee to the test.

Years in the USA and Canada put a brake on imaginative indulgences. Dollars allow little room for dreaming. Young countries with crystal clear air and sharply defined outlines deal with hard-boiled facts, not with wonders a misty climate may conceal behind its many veils.

Anyhow, I plump for the Fairies and the Little People— before I get that wild dog back on the leash again. God bless the Little People! I like them because, in the first place, they are always young and do not grow old; because they are gay and happy and full of dancing and song; because they are ready for intercourse of a limited sort with the human race—mischievous it may be, but always ready to play with us—under certain conditions. My imaginative tenet in my Imaginative Creed remains an item in a creed of starry wonder, attractive to other escapists besides myself. I listen to the "Horns of Elfland faintly blowing"—or hear the tired human call:

Oh, Fairies, take me out of this dull world,
For I would ride with you upon the wind,
Run on the top of the dishevelled tide,
And dance upon the mountains like a flame.

If that cry doesn't ring a bell somewhere inside you, nothing will.[5]

Yet there is danger in the offing: intercourse between the two worlds, our world of Time and theirs of Eternity. Keep your dog carefully on the leash! If you admit one of these friendly Little People into your flat—or, rather, your highland croft, and let yourself be "touched"—well, you're a goner. For they want to entice you into their own happier region:

"I kiss you—and the world begins to fade," cries the intruder, and the human child is lost to her home and parents . . . And so, thinking of Thomas the Rhymer and others, I wonder endlessly what they experienced and where they went.[6]

Now, talking of the Little People, Fairies especially, it must be clearly stated that I have no truck at all with those horrible little monstrosities with wings and spangled tights that were once presented to us in photographs backed by names of authority. Of the origin of these horrible pictures, I know nothing. Yet I well remember being shown snapshots of children playing in a leafy glade with "fairies" sprinkled everywhere among the branches.[7] In common with the other monstrosities I have mentioned, they all seemed to have escaped from some suburban pantomime. And I recall a moment of embarrassment when, pointing to the play of speckled sunlight and shadow, among the leaves, I ungallantly discovered a number more. They were literally all over the place.

A point in favour of their existence, too, is that people who swear to have caught glimpses of them scurrying and flitting about on their lawful occasions, are never frightened. They cause excitement, admiration, but never fear. How crude the ghost is in comparison! Prefaced by a queer sense of cold, there follows automatically a stirring at the roots of the hair, or rather of the old pores where hair once grew, down the spine. We go through the protective performance of trying to look as big and fierce as we can.

As, indeed, the cat still does. The scalp, similarly, tingles. Yes, we are still as close to our primitive animal origins as that—still afraid of the dark. Our spines and scalps rehearse the ancient formula. We still talk of hair-raising stories, of "pricking up" our ears like the fox and the hare. And a vein of superstition persists, I think, in every mother's son of us.

But the Little People, God bless 'em, bring no terror with them. Tears, maybe, but mostly the laughter and yearning that belongs to those who never grow old; mischievous gaiety perhaps, but in any case, nothing malignant, and surely just the right sort of folk to invite and play with at Xmas time.

Yes, but there's something bigger than this mere chat about Fairies and the Little People. Much bigger—if perhaps less credible. I recall my first meeting with that phantasmagoria of the gorgeous East—the Deva Evolution, so called. For its charm and wonder take the breath away.

The Deva Evolution—Deva meaning goddess—thrilled my early years. Whether I came across it in the *Vedas* or the *Upanishads* hardly matters—it described a non-human Evolutionary System that runs parallel to our Human Evolution, yet without intercourse between the two.[8] A gulf seems fixed. It spread over a vast field. Beginning with what we call Fairies or the Little People, it was concerned, in its lowest functions, with the operations of what we call Nature: the structure of flowers, the growth of crystals, the formation of snow-crystals . . . and thence, passing upwards into larger configurations, even through Greek Gods and Angels, into the region of Planetary Spirits. It presented an enticing and fabulous explanation of what you and I call Natural Law.

Only these Natural Laws did not operate automatically. Oh no. They operated faultlessly because they were attended to by these minute Intelligences. Now, isn't that a delightful idea? I ask you. When you watch a primrose unfolding, or a complicated snow-flake becoming a formation of sparkling wonder on your windowsill, isn't it an entrancing wonder to think of a busy little Intelligence rather than a dull Law of Nature?

Well, if this seems nonsense, just stretch your imagination a bit, and think of this other Eastern possibility . . . this Deva Evolution.

From which—now, take a deep breath and admit we don't know everything—what about the conception of Fechner, the Leipzig scientist who blazed upon the world his dazzling idea that our Earth—yes, our dull, dead Earth—might be conceivably the body of some higher consciousness . . . in other words, a living entity.[9] Who can define what a body is? Fantastic and absurd you say. Yet Fechner, as reported by William James in his *Plurality of Worlds*, made out a striking case. It makes you think, at any rate, if you can think—and think, open-mindedly.

The sea has its fish, the air its birds, the earth its animals and humans—what has the Ether, that apparently universal element? His answer is, "The Heavenly Bodies". That takes your breath away. Yet Fechner sets these Heavenly Bodies as higher in the scale than our poor human structures— merely a heavy mass with a few limbs protruding. They have the perfect shape—a circle. They are self-contained— they need nothing outside themselves, whereas we humans must go outside ourselves for food, heat and air. They stand in perfect equipoise with their neighbours in space. They belong to a higher type of consciousness than the human.

Fechner's case has to be read to be believed. It's too long to elaborate. At any rate, it stretches the imagination. Let's leave it at that. A stretched imagination, I hold, is good for the soul. Personally, I come back to my delightful Little People. That is quite a stretch in itself . . . enough for most people anyhow . . . and if you don't believe me, ask the children. With them, at any rate, the sense of wonder hasn't atrophied.

25 December 1948.

Notes

[1] This oft-quoted phrase comes from Yeats's verse-drama *The Countess Kathleen* (1892), first performed in 1899. The play concerns the Countess who sells her soul to the Devil to save her tenants from starvation during a famine. The full quote, spoken by Oona, Countess Kathleen's foster-mother, is "The years like great black oxen tread the world, and God the herdsman, goads them on behind . . . "

[2] The society Blackwood refers to is the Hermetic Order of the Golden Dawn. W. B. Yeats (1865-1939) had been initiated into this in March 1890. I do not know when Blackwood first met Yeats, but it must have been soon after he returned from New York in March 1899. Although Yeats's interest in Theosophy had waned it may be through the Theosophical Society that his and Blackwood's paths crossed. Blackwood had already been a member of the society in the Toronto branch and again in New York, and he had joined the London lodge in May 1899. Yeats initiated Blackwood into the Golden Dawn on 30 October 1900.

[3] I don't know when Blackwood first met George Russell (1867-1935). His mystical treatise, *The Candle of Vision*, was published in 1918 so the meeting must have been after that, but Blackwood rarely travelled to Ireland and Russell did not move to England until 1932. Blackwood

was certainly in Northern Ireland in 1925, and Russell spent much time in adjacent Donegal, but I suspect their meeting must have been earlier if *The Candle of Vision* was fresh in his mind, so probably soon after the end of the Great War.

[4] Yeats had died in Menton in France, a place Blackwood knew well, and was buried near there at Roquebrun-Cap-Martin. However, his remains were moved to Drumcliff, Co. Sligo, almost in the shadow of Ben Bulben, in September 1948, only three months before Blackwood gave this talk.

[5] "The Horns of Elfland" is from the poem *The Princess* (1847) by Alfred, Lord Tennyson, but the quatrain that follows is from Yeats's 1894 play *The Land of Heart's Desire*.

[6] Thomas the Rhymer was a Scottish laird who lived in the thirteenth century and was noted for his prophecies. In the century after his death a legend developed into a ballad about him being abducted by the Queen of Elfland and returned with the gift of prophecy. The ballad became best known in the version expanded by Sir Walter Scott in *Minstrelsy* in 1803.

[7] Blackwood is referring to the Cottingley Fairies, which two children purportedly photographed in 1917, and again in 1920, and which Sir Arthur Conan Doyle was duped into believing were real.

[8] Blackwood almost certainly came across the concept of Deva Evolution through his studies of Theosophy. It fascinated him all his life and became part of his philosophy about the world of Nature. He used it most potently in

The Bright Messenger (1921), the sequel to *Julius LeVallon* (1916), in which LeVallon's son, Julian, has both a human and a non-human elemental spirit. Julian realises that the world is not yet ready for him to exploit his Non-Human role.

[9] Gustav Fechner (1801-1887) was a German philosopher and physicist who was also a pioneer in psychology. He developed the idea that the Earth, like humans and all of creation, had a soul and that the projection of the Earth's spirit took the form of the early gods and mythical creatures. Effectively it gave the concept of Mother Earth a philosophical basis. The idea has since been resurrected by James Lovelock as the Gaia principle. Blackwood used Fechner's theory as the basis for his novel *The Centaur* in 1911.

The Birth of an Idea

If you possess the virtue, or the vice, of writing fantastic tales, sooner or later someone is sure to ask you: "Where on earth did you get that idea from? What in the world made you think of it?" The answer is that you did not think of it. It flashed into the mind apparently out of nothing. Thinking, hard thinking, helped to shape the story later, but the idea itself was not the result of thought.

I am not thinking of the novelist who takes his material from human life direct, historical or nearer home, but of the writers who deal in fantasy, into whose mind flashes suddenly some wild, incredible idea. Where do they come from, these chancy, wayward ideas? What is their origin? One cannot trace any line of approach for they flash up, assault the imagination, set it on fire, and then vanish. They have been lying in wait, making no sign, giving no hint, until something touches off the fuse.

Are these ideas inspirational in character? It looks like it. Inspiration is a big, often a noble word: but it is the technique, not the quality, that interests me at this moment. An inspiration may be valuable, or it may be worthless; but it is the birth, the genesis of an idea of this kind that I want to find an explanation for. These ideas burst in the brain like a shooting star: from what strange storehouse do they shoot?

These are questions which perhaps I cannot answer, but many years ago a friend gave an answer that at least made me think. He was an eminent medical man with interests far outside his immediate work, such as physical research, abnormal psychology and the rest. He was then the editor of *Brain*.[1] The conversation was about artists and their gifts, and whether these gifts enable them to be more aware of things than ordinary people. And as I was beginning to scribble myself, he naturally picked on writing. "Writing!" he exclaimed. "Oh, writing is a function like any other natural operation. Yes, writing is merely functional."

Well, what this doctor said was a "talking point", as Elgar used to say sometimes, his eyes twinkling at me sideways while he sat at the piano playing some lovely songs for a bad children's play of mine.[2] And my medical friend thus elaborated his meaning as we developed the point. "The average man," he suggested, "receives only a few impressions every minute, whereas the sensitive high-strung type we call the artist receives them in an enormously higher ratio. Vivid impressions pour in upon him all day in a rapid flood—from light, colour, sound, form and all the rest. These impressions never cease; indeed, they swamp him. He becomes packed to overflowing, his mind is overfed and he must get rid of these impressions somehow. Purge himself of this undigested mass of material. If, luckily, this artist has some talent for expression, sooner or later out it all comes. If you care to put it that way, his talent is a purgative. Writing, as I say, is functional."

I remember how he developed and emphasised this point. "These impressions," he went on, never really get lost. They may be forgotten by the conscious mind, but they are not lost and they are not dead, and therefore, of course, they are not really forgotten, either. They have just gone below, that is all. They may evidently be out of immediate reach, that is to say, cannot at once be brought to mind, but they are not inaccessible. Stewing in their own juice, so to speak, these impressions lie hidden, but waiting in that appalling storehouse of varied odds and ends which we are told is the subconscious or, even perhaps, according to Jung, the general unconscious mind. Yes, there they are, fairies or monsters as may be the case, undigested mostly, but by no means always inert. Indeed, they may even mature and pass into something rich and strange before suddenly flashing into the normal consciousness like a star, and clamouring for recognition and expression. They are summoned, evoked, it seems, by the most trivial details of a walk down the street or by something seen in a room; but sometimes they force their way up through the turmoil of some confusing dream, when the surface consciousness lies quiet.

This congested region of the mind seems to be the largely uncharted ocean which inspiration draws upon for its occasionally radiant supply of ideas. The popular simile, of course, is that of the iceberg with so much more below the surface than above, and it is, after all, a good one.

Now, as to these ideas that do not lie inert, but ripen and then appear in developed shape, there is some evidence to suggest that these were caused by impressions that came first with a strong emotion, a thrill, and that this vivid emotion, after it has been piled away below, slowly dramatises itself. It may return as a story or a lyric in complete, even dramatic form. During the day, for example, a strong emotion may be stirred in the artist by a sunset, a snatch of music, a blossoming tree, a bird's song, anything that wakens real yearning, for to the artist the most common experience is enough to do this. This yearning, stirred by Beauty, is intensively alive and active for a short time, then it slowly fades, until it finally dies away and is forgotten. That is the kind of thrill, I think, which frustrated in the surface consciousness and denied expression, is apt to reappear in a dramatised form long afterwards. It may, as I said, be worthless or valuable, but the technique is inspirational. Perhaps the genius knows how to draw upon this inexhaustible supply at will, and with supreme powers of selection; whilst the artist of whom we say that his muse is dead, has perhaps lost touch with his subconscious. Whether that lost touch can be recovered, deliberately regained by conscious effort, is an extremely interesting and pregnant question which one would like to explore. Methods do exist, I believe, but they are not easy ones.

In Jung's valuable little book, *Essays on Contemporary Events* [1947], he briefly mentions how his study of various German patients in the years when Hitler was moving slowly to power, revealed hints that dreadful things, even then, were boiling up in their unconscious minds. Chaos, turmoil, cruelty, sadism, a reversion to old pagan gods, and heaven knows what else besides he noted in his examinations. He foresaw, indeed he foretold, an outburst of an extraordinary and terrifying kind as probable if this latent accumulation of mental disorder ever rose to the surface and found expression. Himself a Swiss, and probably the most penetrating and comprehensive psychologist in the world today, he took this set of German patients as a cross-section of the German race; and he felt that, although at the moment they remained dumb, if they were once provided with the vehicle of a voice, the whole awful torrent would rush up and out. Then Hitler, himself a neurotic, above all a medium, provided the voice. Yes, Hitler was a medium as definitely as any one of low intellectual type who runs a séance room. Hitler provided the voice for the entire German unconscious, that unconscious from which his power derived because he expressed its own atrocious disorder.

To return to this notion of sudden ideas leaping out from that underground storehouse which is the unconscious. One has read in countless solemn volumes the analysis of this "inspirational technique", as I choose to call it; but it was much more interesting to observe, as I once did, the process happening to myself. Years ago in Egypt, too absorbed in writing a book to think of other work, I woke one morning with a sentence running in my head: "You will drown, yet will not know you drown." It was a meaningless sentence that I felt must belong to a dream, the rest of which had vanished; but it went on so persistently that I became convinced a story of sorts lay behind it—that it was, in fact, the climax to something which lay already complete in my subconscious.

Now, effort to recover a lost dream is useless; no effort will do it. Either it comes back to memory, or it does not. In this perhaps trivial example—for, as I said, inspiration is no criterion for value—one thing did come back to my memory. It was a dreadful tale, told in my hearing some weeks before, of a man who died of thirst in the desert. It had moved me deeply, it had thrilled me, for it was true; and though the tale itself was more or less forgotten in detail, the emotion of horror and distress which I had felt had sunk out of sight, but was waiting to be used. And in this case it did not lie long inert. It had dramatised itself in that kind of sequence we call a story, and had now suddenly emerged tail first, so to speak, with its climax running in my head. At any rate, this is how my imaginative temperament chose to regard it as a possible explanation to the mystery.

So I went to my typewriter, not to struggle with the book that had been absorbing me, but with the idea to attempt some commonplace little short story that would justify and explain that absurd sentence: "You will drown, yet will not know you drown."

I had not the faintest idea how to start about it, though I knew that once a framework was found the rest would probably follow. After a time a scenario of sorts eventually suggested itself. It was some nonsense about a boy and a girl in love, and gradually the tale germinated. As the windows of the room where I was, looked out over the desert, the background to my story was, of course, a desert. Details would be boring, but the story seemed to run smoothly enough—it was published later in the old *Westminster Gazette*—but until I was quite near the end I had no idea, at least no clear idea, how that queer sentence was going to justify itself. And then, suddenly, it did justify itself, and the story was complete. I am inclined to believe that it had lain dormant, but complete, down below, waiting for expression; and the strong emotion surrounding it had kept it alive and active, so that it insisted on being expressed. But the daily surface consciousness of my mind had been far too occupied with its clamorous affairs to take any notice; so it had shot up from the unconscious with some vehemence when that surface consciousness lay quiescent in sleep. I caught it by the tail just by chance. Perhaps after all my medical friend was right. Writing is functional, merely a pill, a purge.[3]

A more striking case perhaps of this "inspirational" theory of a powerful emotion dramatising itself eventually in story form occurred after a journey I made through the Caucasus. The stupendous grandeur of those almost legendary mountains made a profound impression upon a young and sensitive mind.[4] After the Isles of Greece, Smyrna, Athens, the Golden Horn, what a climax it was to land in Batoum, the Colchis of the Argonauts and the Golden Fleece, and to pass by way of Tiflis into Shelley's vale of "awful loveliness", where Prometheus became unbound. After an extended tour I came home charged with a thousand storms of beauty and wonder, only to find that I could not write a line about it all. Stunned and bewildered by what I had seen, the mind was speechless, incapable of expressing anything beyond a few superficial travel sketches. Indeed a year passed without even a desire to write about it until suddenly, one night in a filthy London fog, I caught a sound outside my closed window. It was a sound which seemed to me ravishing, yes, it was intoxicating music. Then I realised what after all it really was, only some wretched fellow playing on his penny whistle in the dark Soho street. Yet, in that instant, as I listened, the whole glory of the legendary Caucasus flamed back over me with its haunting wonder and majesty as though, in a rush of fire. That penny whistle—Pan's pipes, if they ever sounded anywhere in this mechanical world— lit up and vitalised that filthy street and, indeed, the whole sordid vale of humans. I cannot explain it, it happened, and that is all I know.

I ran downstairs and gave the vagabond some money— something that, as they say in the Old Kent Road, knocked him silly. Perhaps it was all my weekly earnings, for all I remember. Then I rushed back into my room and to my writing-table. A flood had been let loose in me, its origin apparently the trivial detail of a wheezy penny whistle. It all stormed up out of the subconscious, and I began a book, a book that, good or bad, released the dramatised emotions of my journey a year before the Caucasus. And it was a book which, as they say, "wrote itself". It was called *The Centaur*.[5]

3 March 1948.

Notes

[1] Blackwood was probably talking about Sir Henry Head (1861-1940) who was editor of *Brain* from 1905 to 1921. Blackwood rarely provided information to identify living people but as Head had died in 1940 he'd have felt able to allude to him.

[2] This would have been *The Starlight Express* (1916), which Blackwood and composer Sir Edward Elgar (1857-1934) based on Blackwood's novel *A Prisoner in Fairyland* (1913).

[3] It seems strange that in this essay Blackwood did not name the story. It was "By Water", published in the *Westminster Gazette* on 18 April 1914, as he recalled, and included in *Day and Night Stories*.

[4] "Young" is a relative term. Blackwood was forty-one when he ventured to the Caucasus.

[5] *The Centaur* was published in November 1911, and Blackwood had wrestled with a writer's block about the story, incorporating that struggle in the story "Imagination" published in the *Westminster Gazette* for 17 December 1910, just a few months after his return from the Caucasus.

Our Former Lives

The alleged recovery of memories of former lives always has a special appeal for millions who are interested in reincarnation; and I use the word "alleged" because I think some of the claims are often too easily accepted. Those of us who have read Professor Flournoy's *From India to the Planet Mars* [1900], with its sensational account of Hélène Smith's memory of her earlier life on Mars, and the experiences of Col. De Rochas when he was conducting research into possible pre-natal memory, may be more cautious before wholesale and uncritical acceptance of such evidence.

An interesting case of recovery once came my way and may be worth telling. As it concerns a book of my own, *Julius LeVallon* [1916], I hope I shall be forgiven for mentioning it when I add that, being now out of print, there is no advantage to myself. It is a study of reincarnation, the title character based on the Hindu medical student whom I knew in Edinburgh.

The story includes certain scenes I must briefly allude to, the first being a description of a Sun Worship ritual round a great, smooth dome in a desert. Round this dome, as dawn is about to break over the vast expanse of sand, a concourse of people stand waiting for the sunrise. All are wearing robes of various colours, the colours of the spectrum, and gradually they sort themselves out according to these colours till they stand motionless at last in circles round the dome. Each ring has its particular colour and is perhaps ten figures deep. They stand absolutely still and silent. Then, as the sun shows its first piercing ray over the rim of the horizon, they begin to move, the innermost ring to the right, the next to the left, the third again to the right and so on until the whole mass of worshippers show these concentric rings of colour in a huge single wheel. And as they move, each ring chants the particular note appropriate to its colour, so that a vast choral song rises in greeting to the now visible sun. This strange, even magnificent picture rose vividly before me as I attempted to describe it.

The second scene describes how, after battle, the prisoners were made to stand on a narrow ledge inside a great circular building. The ledge sloped towards the deep space below. It provided just room enough for the prisoner to hold a precarious balance with difficulty. On the ground far below, their sharp points uppermost, spears were planted. Some of the prisoners balanced as long as they could, then fell to their cruel death; others preferred to cut their anguish short, and jumped instantly.

The origin of these two scenes I do not know; they just rose vividly in my mind as I was writing; they seemed to me as convincing as though I had witnessed them. Imagination? Yes, of course; though some believe that Imagination is Memory, as we all know.

So I come now to the case of recovery of memories mentioned above, for it is related to these two scenes.

A letter from a stranger arrived one day, the writer explaining that he was especially interested in my book *Julius LeVallon*, and would like to meet me if possible; he said he was a Staff Captain in the Australian army, his regiment being at the moment in Egypt. Certain experiences, he mentioned, that had come his way pointed to the possibility that they were memories of earlier lives; he would like to discuss them with me. And, after a considerable interval, when I happened to be in Bordighera, he came over from Mentone and we spent an afternoon together.

He was by no means the gullible or credulous type, but a hard-headed, efficient officer, with the physical counterpart of an athlete and a clear, well-equipped mind, and I became more and more interested as I listened to his story.

Back in Australia, he told me, he was a travelling salesman in tea, covering great distances inland to reach outlying, lonely places. Since early youth he had been a firm believer in reincarnation, feeling very strongly, without quite knowing why, that one of his previous lives had been in ancient Egypt. It had not been a specially distinguished life, but it had been connected, probably in some minor capacity, with the priesthood or, at any rate, with the temple life. Few books on the subject had come his way, but the little he had managed to read on the subject brought with it a strange sense of familiarity. It all attracted him enormously, and one of his great hopes was that some day he would be able to visit Egypt and see the land of his dreams at first hand. But life as a traveller in tea offered little enough chance of that, until, having enlisted in the war, his regiment in due course went to Europe and eventually was ordered to Egypt. His dream was coming true.

I asked him about his sensations and first impressions, to which he replied that it "was just like coming home after a very long interval. And the first striking thing I noticed," he added, "was that since I was last there, the Nile had changed its bed."

It is doubtless true, of course, that the Nile has changed its bed more than once in the many thousand years of its existence, especially from Assouan or Wady Halfa downwards, though I did not take any steps myself to look up what records there might be to support his claim. Nor could I follow precisely the rather detailed account of the changed bed he gave. Knowing Egypt well, I just listened to his story with growing interest, as he went on to tell me of queer vivid memories he had of the building of the pyramids at Mena, and of the quarrying of the sandstone blocks from the Mokhattan Hills not far from Cairo; also of the road that was constructed from the river up the steep slopes where the pyramids now stand. And, as I listened, I kept thinking of Kipling's "Greatest Story in the World" in which the love-sick bank clerk chatted about his memories as a galley slave; the parallel was striking. As for the priesthood and the temple life, the officer thought that must have come much later in a subsequent existence.

In reply to questions, he talked a good deal, too, about the sinister feelings the old temples stirred in him, the Temple of the Sphinx, especially, and the Valley of the Tombs of the Kings near Thebes, the present Luxor. The rituals and magic of the priesthood aimed at power, but not power of an exalted kind, and a residue of former practices could still be felt by anyone sensitive enough to receive such impressions, as though their aftermath still emanated from the granite and sandstone blocks that had witnessed the potent rituals of long ago.

We talked and talked together until the sun went down into the blue Mediterranean, and then, before he left for his train, he told me another rather singular incident that brought in beauty.

It was in connection with his conviction that the ghostly emanations of ancient times still cling to the ancient land; but in this incident, it was Isis, the benevolent, that touched his sense of worship. He was spending a few days leave, he told me, in Luxor, and he used his last day visiting the shops and booths in search for something he left unmentioned at first. It was a long and difficult search, apparently, but by evening he had filled a big sack with its results, whatever they were. Towards midnight, he hired a donkey, one of the powerful Egyptian donkeys all tourists know so well, and sallied forth under the brilliant stars towards the desolate hills. A track leads over the arid waste of stones, mounting slowly to the three thousand feet summit, which in due course he reached. No one was about, he did not see a living soul, and on top of the ridge he dismounted and waited patiently for the dawn.

No one who has seen the stars fade slowly out of that marvellous Egyptian night sky, as the first signs of dawn creep over the eastern horizon, can ever forget it. It comes in the end so suddenly, so swiftly. The light first steals over the distant Lybian desert, glints from the quiet Nile, tips the houses of Luxor far below, the imposing mass of the huge Karnak temple, and then the sun comes up with a sort of magnificent rush. But before it actually appeared, the officer unloaded his precious sack from the donkey's back, opened it, and stood ready. Then as the first rays lit the world, he turned it upside down and let its contents flow in a cataract of colour over the ground—hundreds of red roses. It was his offering to Isis, the offering of a devout worshipper.

I have left to the last the matter of the two strange scenes described earlier, though he spoke of them long before his account of his Egyptian memories. He asked me almost at once how I knew about the two vivid pictures my book described and from whence they were derived; but I could only tell him that while writing the book they just rose in my mind. Whereupon he told me with intense conviction, his sincerity at any rate unquestionable, that he definitely *remembered* both scenes. He had been present, he had witnessed them. He had stood worshipping the sun in a coloured robe; he had also, if much earlier still, stood among the prisoners of war on that awful ledge, then leaped to his death on the spears below. And when I had to insist that I had not been favoured with any personal memory myself, and that it was just imagination, he repeated, with a shrug of his shoulders, "But, of course, imagination *is* memory—isn't it?"

It is difficult to convey in cold print the positive conviction that lay in this officer's soul. In any case, such partial glimpses of recovered memory as he claimed seemed to me more authentic, probably, than long detailed accounts I have so often heard of having been a King, a Queen, or some great historical character, where the Law of Compensation offers escape from a life of humble drudgery Today to the glories of some distinguished Past.

May 1947.

The Fire Body

Are persons with a definite delusion more numerous, perhaps, than we suppose, persons sane and normal in their reactions to all the stimuli of daily life yet entirely, even gravely, deluded on some one particular point?

It was my experience with the Fire Body that raised the question in my mind, and so persistently that I began a thorough and careful investigation of my own special field of weakness. Such a search, of course, however honestly undertaken, can only lead to one conclusion, namely that any genuine delusion, no matter how gross and outstanding, could never seem a delusion to its possessor. To an outsider alone would it appear as such. Yet an outsider who dared point it out would appear to its possessor as himself deluded, speaking therefore without authority, his reward merely a pitying smile. A real cure can only come from the same source as the delusion—from within oneself.

The lady who introduced me to the Fire Body (my own) was as normal, wholesome, charming and cultured as any I have ever met. She discussed Greek sculpture, winter sports, horses, stock market speculation, music and literature as sensibly as she discussed this Fire Body. All these, I mean, lay in the same plane of reality and actuality as the Fire Body. She did not regard a Fire Body as an exceptional or abnormal object of perception, beyond that it was not, certainly, as commonly known as most things.

Though difficult of access, it was not supernatural. It was, to her, as literally real as her gain or loss of one-eighth, or her hearing of Holst and Scriabin.

The esoterically learned will forgive a few words of preliminary explanation to clear the ground, so to speak, and make what follows intelligible. My explanation may not be strictly orthodox or accurate, for my acquaintance with this particular branch of lore is scanty. From desultory reading of various queer volumes, however, the vague imaginative surmise lay in me that the elements were once regarded as the field of activity, if not the actual clothing, of certain sub-human beings. The four elements of mediæval superstition seem a trifle out of date at a time when science admits to several score of them, yet some Rosicrucian glamour formerly shed its strange haunting twilight upon the notion that Earth, Air, Fire and Water represented precisely such fields of activity and that each was inhabited by its own special denizens. Gnomes, sylphs, undines and salamanders, to say nothing of "Elementals" in general were, if not actual entities, at least Powers of a sort to conjure with.

In these sub-human regions, moreover, the Soul could likewise function and adventure, though not in its ordinary waking consciousness. It must use the appropriate vehicle of Body, of which vehicles or Bodies it possessed the requisite four. The Earth Body was the only one the majority knew about, but Air, Water and Fire Bodies were there for those whose special knowledge or training enabled them to function in them. Leaving their Earth Bodies in sleep or unconsciousness, these few, assuming one or other of the three vehicles according to desire, might adventure in strange airy, watery or fiery heavens.

Some such imaginative faith apparently enriched the private mental life of the charming woman who introduced me to my own Fire Body; something of this kind of lore, at any rate, lay behind the little episode that follows.

There is no need to remind ourselves at this time of the portentous farce of Johanna Southcott and her ludicrous "Box", at the opening of which twenty-four bishops, according to the conditions laid down by the Seeress, were to be present.[1] Its opening, "when England was in peril", having been delayed for well over a hundred years, if I remember rightly, was to reveal the means for saving the old country; so when a friend mentioned, "I'm going to the Sesame Club, and you had better come along with me," adding that the occasion was a meeting to consider the immediate opening of the famous Box, possibly its opening then and there, I accepted with all the curiosity of an old New York newspaper reporter.[2] My friend, as a member, led me in; we were already late; the lecture room, where the ceremony was to take place, I found crowded to the ceiling—with women. Not a black coat or a tweed coat was to be seen. I recall standing a moment on the threshold with my hostess, glancing quickly round at the packed rows of women and whispering, while I turned nervously to scuttle out, "This is no place for me—I'm off!" At which moment precisely I heard my name rather breathlessly spoken just behind me and, turning, saw an acquaintance, Miss T., confronting me.

She was rather breathless with forcing her way down from an upper row.

"I'm so glad I just caught you!" she exclaimed, catching, metaphorically at least, my coat-tails. "There's a woman here who's dying to meet you. Says she simply *must*. A friend of mine. She was sitting next to me when she saw you . . . !"

I edged towards the hall. "But—er—why, exactly?"

"Most extraordinary thing," pursued Miss T., pursuing me at the same time into the club vestibule, "but she's just seen you standing there with all your four Bodies, all in a row, side by side. She hasn't the faintest notion of your name or who you are."

"My four Bodies, you said?"

"Your Earth Body she has never set eyes on. It's one of the others she suddenly recognised—your Fire Body. She's known it for ten years. Known it intimately, she says. She's dying to meet you. I gave her your name, but she'd never heard of it."

"How," I stammered, "where—when—has she met it—me?"

Miss T. looked earnestly at me. My escaping step hesitated. I was intrigued to say the least.

"Oh, I know nothing of all that," she explained. "She was sitting next to me, when you stepped inside the doorway and looked round the room. You were only there a minute when she nudged me excitedly and whispered: 'There he is! My God!' and pointed. I looked in the direction of her finger and said, 'But that's a man I know—a Mr. Blackwood.' Then she jumped up and cried: 'Oh, do introduce me. I know his Fire Body,' or 'I knew him *in* his Fire Body. I've been out with him for years, ten years at least, but I hadn't a notion who it was. He used to teach me things, all sorts of things. Oh, please, please introduce me to him before he goes. He's going already!' So, please," urged Miss T., "*do* stay a moment and I'll fetch her down!"

She disappeared, leaving me in the vestibule, feeling half intrigued, half foolish. Slightly bewildered, too. A strange atmosphere of expectancy had already been evoked by the mixed vision of England's peril, Johanna Southcott, the weird seeress of a century and a half ago, the fluttering lawn sleeves of twenty-four ghostly Bishops hovering in the background, and now, in addition to all this, the splendid dream that I possessed—visibly—three bodies in addition to my familiar physical one. And this in the Sesame Club in Dover Street, London, W.1, in the twentieth century.[3]

I remember looking round me for something to lean upon in more senses than one. People were still crowding in to hear about the box; but my hostess, a cynical, matter-of-fact lady was already in her seat, listening to the chairwoman, Mrs. Fox, I think, who was now opening the proceedings.[4] My eye rested with satisfaction, I remember, upon the portly hall porter, who was most certainly of this world—when Miss T.'s voice again startled me: "Oh, I'm so glad you're still here," she was saying more breathlessly than before, "for I've brought my friend down. She wants so much to meet you."

And I was introduced forthwith to a charming, good-looking woman of perhaps thirty-three, who stared at me with keen interest and a distinctly scrutinising and critical expression. Her calm appealed to me from the first; she was dignified, quiet, self-possessed. She said what she had to say once, not twice. After a brief apology for forcing an introduction in this way, and a word of thanks to me for waiting, she expressed her pleasure and her interest at meeting me—"at last".

"When I told Miss T.," she said, "I didn't know your name, I was mistaken. At first, in my excitement, I didn't connect you with the books—I *have* read one of your books. But what interests me," she continued with a stark honesty I admired and appreciated, "was that I saw your figure standing in the porch with three other figures beside it, and that one of those figures I had known for years. I have felt, and still feel," she added quietly, "a deep, deep gratitude towards it. Until this minute I had no idea who it was."

In the slight pause that came I asked *what* the figure was, and *why* she felt this gratitude.

Before answering me, she looked about for a seat. I reminded her that the meeting had begun and that Johanna's Box might possibly be opened while we chatted in the vestibule.

"I'd rather talk with you," she replied, and led me to a sofa in the guests' waiting-room. "The 'figure'," she began, "was undoubtedly a Fire Body—someone in his Fire Body. I know," she went on with quiet conviction, "because I myself am Fire."

I made no comment, and she continued in her even, gentle voice: "You know," she explained, "for *of course* you do—that we all have the Four Elements in us, Earth, Air, Fire and Water. One of them, however, predominates. An individual is thus one of them—an Earth, Air, Fire or Water person. Your horoscope and the Zodiac easily determine this. A Fire person and a Water person never get on—they extinguish each other, while Air and Fire people, on the other hand, stimulate each other. A Fire person will never come to grief by fire, nor a Water person drown—their instinct preserves them. But, *of course*, you know all this, because you have written about it in your books—"

"So, you are Fire," I put in quickly.

"I am Fire, yes," she assured me, "and I know a Fire Body when I see one—naturally. I travel in my Fire Body every night in sleep. That's how I met yours. You, too, are Fire—though, I judge, Air and Fire, too."

"And why," I asked, sticking to my original question, "does that make you feel grateful? For you mention gratitude just now."

She paused a minute or two before replying. "Because," she said at length, gravely, "you—you in your Fire Body— have taught me such wonderful things."

I stared blankly at her.

"Amazing, marvellous things," she added quietly, yet with intense admiration. "I can never, *never*, be grateful enough for your guidance, help, instruction. On more than one occasion you have saved my life. The help you gave was above rubies."

I sat there speechless—in the vestibule of the Sesame Club in Dover Street in the twentieth century; but a moment later, having recovered my self-possession, when I proceeded to inquire the nature of this help, how and where we met, what words I spoke, and a few other practical details I wanted to know about, she remarked quietly: "If you will come to tea tomorrow I will try and tell you a little more about it, if you don't mind and will forgive—I find this atmosphere difficult to talk in—unsympathetic." She indicated the fact that neighbours were listening to us. There was certainly a lack of privacy.

She rose, and I rose with her, naturally. I made many apologies for having detained her. I promised to come to tea—it was a flat in Albemarle Street, next door and on the top floor. I made a note of the number and the following day I arrived punctually at the hour appointed.

We resumed our conversation practically where it had been interrupted. The flat, I noticed, was cosy and delightful, the cakes and China tea were of the best. It was the flat of a cultured woman—lined bookshelves, pictures, sculpture, a piano smothered with music, the best weeklies lying about, serious books everywhere—a flat untidy, lived-in, human, and alert to all the movements of the day. Evidences of an up to date and wide intelligence were obvious enough. And they were natural. First-rate drawings of famous horses, too, I noticed, with various splendid photographs of Greek sculpture, water colours of Paestum, Pompeii streets, and some lovely reproductions of Florentine masterpieces.

Under the broad mantelpiece I saw a few indifferent watercolours of Alpine scenery, samples of winter-sport adventure, skiing and the like, and among these one painting in particular that caught my eye. Why this particular painting attracted me I can not explain; the point is that it did so. I kept looking at it, while my hostess talked. It interested me, it *drew* my attention. For some reason I wanted to know more about it. It would be only too easy to assert, in view of what was told me later, that it seemed familiar, dramatic too. Yet that would not be strictly true. The strict truth is stated when I say that it interested me—apart from any intrinsic merit. For it was merely a commonplace, distinctly amateur watercolour of a youth with flaming red hair which stood up as though blown by a wind, the face and features ordinary enough, yet with something in the eyes, and in the eyes alone, that startled. Yet the idea arose in me that I had seen it somewhere before. It was in this vague notion that the sense of familiarity doubtless arose. I must add that no evidence can possibly support this notion. I had never seen it before, I have never seen anything like it since.

Sufficient, then, for the moment, that I kept looking at it with particular interest; and I recall that I intended at the first opportunity to ask what, and whom, it represented. My hostess, meanwhile, was chatting over the tea-cups.

"I was going to tell you about my Fire Body excursions," she resumed calmly our interrupted conversation. "It must be over ten years ago," she went on, "that I first became aware of having unusual dreams. Most of us dream, I know, and some of us"—she smiled understandingly—"think our dreams of importance. I never made that mistake. The first thing that made me take my dreams seriously was that I dreamed so coherently."

"Coherently?" I repeated.

"In the sense," she explained, "that each dream was a sequel to the last one. I met the same person I had met the night before. The talk of the previous night was resumed where I had left off on waking. Sometimes I woke on a question I had asked. The next night that question was answered at once—as though there had been no interruption."

"But the questions and the person?" I ventured. "Were they of interest?"

She stared at me a moment, though I got the impression she looked past me rather than at me. She was thinking. It was not I, as I sat there over my tea-cup, who interested her.

"The questions," she replied gravely, "were of great interest to me, of supreme interest I might say. The person was yourself."

"Myself!" I exclaimed, egotism fixing attention on the point of the person rather than on the nature of the questions.

"You," she stated emphatically and with intense conviction, "but you—not as I see you now. At this actual moment, drinking tea in my flat. It was you in your Fire Body."

I stirred my tea. I thought hard a moment. My temperament and interests were not adverse, not hostile certainly, to any conceivable mental adventure. I had William James, Dr. Osty and countless others, so to speak, at my fingertips. The text books from Charcot to Binet to Féret, to mention no others, poured their accumulated content into my mind. If not hostile, I was certainly advised, and therefore critical. Doubtless, in view of this packed reading and questioning, I was critical in a very real sense.

"In my Fire Body?" I repeated. "You mean, I suppose, that alleged body or vehicle in which our normal consciousness is said to manifest—er—otherwise?"

She gazed at me without comprehension. "I suppose so," she answered, after a considerable pause. "All I know is that I met this figure night after night in my dreams, that it told me wonderful things, that it taught me splendid, amazing teachings and that it was always the same figure—*you*, whom I saw yesterday afternoon for the first time in waking. I saw this figure standing close beside you at the Sesame Club. I saw you in your physical—or Earth—body. Beside you I saw three other figures I did not know or recognise. I recognised only one—the figure I had met so often in dreams—your Fire Body. I was so excited I asked Miss T. who it was."

We both stared hard.

"May I ask," I ventured presently, "*where* we met in your dream? And what the teaching was?" for my tongue refused somehow to ask "what I taught you?" No recollection lay in me of having taught this lady anything, in dream or otherwise. "What kind of thing, for instance?"

Our stare continued for some minutes. My impressions during the little interval were mixed, perhaps, yet one stands out clearly. If any woman told the truth, it was my hostess. She was telling quietly, with intense conviction, something she had indubitably experienced. It was as genuine as her gain or loss in the stock market, as her account of skiing down the Murren Race Track, as her reactions at Paestum or Pompeii. Of that I feel assured.

"*Where?*" she repeated my first question. "Well, it's always the same place. Up a mountain side. You take me up a mountain. It's very steep. Painfully steep. No, you don't take my hand or help me. You lead and I follow. At a certain spot, always the same spot, you just stop. You turn. You don't look at me. You just stand there, looking out and down. An immense landscape stretches below us. You gaze out over it. And—you talk. You tell me things.

You answer my questions. You are kind, patient, but completely indifferent to me—as an individual. You just tell me things I want to know because you know them and I don't. You might be talking to a tree or sheep or stone for all the interest you show in me, myself."

"And—the things we talk about? The questions you ask and I answer?"

She paused again, and again her intense conviction and sincerity came over me. She drew a long breath.

"Marvellous," she whispered. "Perfectly marvellous—and yet so simple that it always mortifies me that I hadn't understood them without asking."

A wild hope flashed through me that I might here find myself on the brink, the perilous uncertain brink, of gathering at least some unusual information snatched, stolen even, from the pregnant subconscious searching of what the text books term a "lucid somnambulist". I caught my breath a moment.

"Tell me," I suggested, using all the combined command and sympathy of eye and voice at my disposal.

She gazed past me as before. She made an effort, a sincere effort, I am convinced. She was trying to think, trying to remember.

"I can't," she said presently, with a sigh. "Try as I will, I can not remember. I only know that what you tell me, what you teach me, affects my whole life. I never can remember what we talk about—never. I only know it guides and helps, and even saves me. My life in the world would collapse but for that help. Yet I never can remember a single detail afterwards. Not one!"

I did not stir my tea; I drank it down.

"The gist of the teaching stays in you, though you recall nothing of the actual words?" I asked presently, putting it as simply as I could.

Waiting for some time before answering, she said it seemed to be something like that perhaps. During the affairs of the day, when she was perplexed, doubtful, uncertain how to act or what to think, an idea would suddenly flash into her. It seemed to come from nowhere, yet it solved her immediate little problem marvellously. And each time this happened there flashed with it a faint haunting memory of some marvellous strange figure belonging to a dream. Not only in daily acts did this occur, but also with her reading, thinking mental life. A puzzle was suddenly resolved, something that perplexed her, simplified, a mental problem in some region of her inner life made clear—and always this same fleeting, vanishing picture of a figure who supplied the solution, then fled before memory could possibly seize or label it. Never could she honestly attribute this help to any other source except the figure of her dream, for she could recall only the figure, and never what the figure had told or taught her. Certainly I detected no attempt to elaborate or justify. She remembered the figure, yet never precisely what the figure said. She attributed the solution of a given problem, mental or otherwise, to the figure merely because each time the sudden guidance and solution came, this flashing memory of the figure darted across her mind.

It was an interesting story. I had to admit that I myself rarely, if ever, dreamed. My dream-content, possibly, she suggested, found vent in my books, and hence my sleep was blameless and uneventful. We talked, or rather I listened, for an hour or more, but my hostess committed herself to nothing I dared label as nonsense, foolish or hysterical. There was no personal encounter of any sort, nor any hint of its possibility even. She was interested in my Fire Body, not in me. She made one or two more than thoughtful comments. "Things we have utterly forgotten and can not place," she mentioned once, "influence the more because we *have* forgotten them. Having utterly forgotten them," she explained, "the will and imagination do not oppose or criticise."

Before I left, on the point of saying good-bye in fact, my eye again caught the little water-colour drawing that had *drawn* my attention so vividly earlier in the afternoon, and I asked what and who it was.

"Oh that," she answered, turning to the picture as I pointed to it. "That," she explained apologetically, "is a little sketch a clairvoyant friend of mine, a girl, did for me. She was here one day and said she saw a figure standing behind me, always. I asked her to draw it. It's you," she said with a smile as I went out. "You in your Fire Body."

She made me a present of it and it hangs on my walls today in a neat black frame.

September 1931.

Notes

[1] Johanna or Joanna Southcott (1750-1814) was a zealously religious woman from Devon who worked on her father's farm and also as a maidservant but who, in her forties, started to have visions of perils that might affect Britain. She became famous in her day and at the time of her death she left a locked box which could only be opened in the presence of twenty-four bishops when Britain was at a moment of dire peril. The box contained prophecies and other items which would deliver Britain from evil. She had a following that continued after her death but the location of the box became uncertain and there were claims by several individuals that they had the real box.

[2] The Sesame Club had been opened in 1895 as a salon that promoted lively discussion of the arts and literature and important topics of the day.

[3] Blackwood does not date this account, but the Sesame Club moved out of its premises in Dover Street during the summer of 1924, so the events he described must have happened in the early 1920s. I do not know the identities of either Miss T. or of his Fire Body hostess.

[4] Rachel Juliet Fox (1858-1939) was a spiritualist who became a Southcottian and first President of the Panacea Society. This had been founded in 1919 to promote the teachings and beliefs of Southcott, and Fox took the lead in contacting the twenty-four bishops to consider when the box should be opened. It had become a serious subject during the Great War and the years immediately after and there were two different occasions in the 1920s when a purported Southcott Box was opened. The first was in April 1925 in Hammersmith when William Mackay, who claimed he owned the true box, opened it without ceremony and with no bishops present. It contained a copy of the New Testament inside of which was a wisp of grey hair, and a piece of parchment apparently written by Southcott and dated 24 December 1805. It was dismissed as a forgery. The well-known ghost hunter Harry Price claimed he had received the box from an unnamed gentleman and prior to its official opening in July 1927 it was x-rayed to reveal its contents which included several scrolls of paper and a pistol. Only one bishop was present. This box was also dismissed as a hoax. I have no evidence that Blackwood attended the Harry Price event which took place at the Hoare Memorial Hall, Westminster. Various claims have since been made about the box which is supposedly in safe keeping with the

Panacea Society. There was a public meeting of the Panacea Society in August 1924 to promote the healing beliefs of Southcott, but this was held at Mortimer Hall in north London, and Blackwood would not have confused it with the Sesame Club.

Passport to the Next Dimension

There are two books that stand out as of the highest value in my life: Hinton's *New Era of Thought* [1888] and P. D. Ouspensky's *Tertium Organum* [1912]. The former was easily accessible, but I only came across the latter about 1921 when Claude Bragdon, whom I did not know, kindly sent me a copy from America. He and Nicholas Bessaraboff were responsible for its translation. I remember reading it with avidity; that it supported and developed Hinton's ideas made it particularly welcome to my seeking mind. His lucid exposition of the different grades of consciousness, showing that as consciousness changes and develops, the sense of space changes and develops too; this and his, to me, new "logic of intuition", made a very special appeal.[1]

There are a few sentences from Bragdon's introduction that may be worth remembering here:

> In naming his book *Tertium Organum*, Ouspensky reveals at a stroke that astounding audacity which characterises his thought throughout . . . Such a title says, in effect: "Here is a book that will re-organise all knowledge." How passing strange, in this era of negative thinking, does such a challenge sound . . . and yet it has the echo in it of something heard before—another volume, Hinton's *A New Era of Thought*.

And Bragdon adds:

> From one point of view this is a terrible book: there
> is a revolution in it—a revolution of the very poles of
> thought. It is a great destroyer of complacency. Yes,
> this is a dangerous book—but then, life is like that.

I wanted to know the author of *Tertium Organum* and
talk with him—yes, and ask him numerous questions. No
useful opening presented itself; I had judged a letter the
wrong approach; I was looking for somebody who knew
him personally. And suddenly this opening came.

I was in Venice on a summer holiday when Lady
Rothermere, whom I knew very slightly, asked me to
lunch and at once said, "There are two people in Paris just
now you ought to know—Ouspensky and Gurdjieff."[2] She
went on to say that the former had come across the latter
in Constantinople and had received special training and
teaching from him. She gave me Gurdjieff's address. We
talked a bit about *Tertium Organum* . . . I cut short my
holiday and left next day for Paris and went straight to see
Gurdjieff in his little flat. The language difference when I
talked with him in that Paris flat proved insurmountable.
French and English were useless; I had no Persian, Russian
or, generally speaking, Caucasian. He suggested a meeting
that afternoon at his headquarters in another part of Paris.
My memories of that meeting with Gurdjieff, helped by
interpreters, though unforgettable, hardly pertain to this
note about Ouspensky, and are therefore omitted.

At the afternoon meeting, however, I came across
Orage, who worked as editor of the *New Age*, and whose
books generally, were familiar to me.[3] And it was through
his good offices that, on returning to London, I began to
attend Ouspensky's meetings in Warwick Gardens.

Orage, whom I knew well, had suggested that Ouspensky, having then settled in London, should hold regular meetings for talk and discussion with a view, I gathered, of sifting out "disciples" (and they were very numerous and from all levels of intelligence) whom he might find ready to go on to Gurdjieff's establishment at Fontainebleau, near Paris. The mere curiosity-seekers were eliminated; those who were told they might go on to Fontainebleau without further delay were, apparently, those who were in earnest and knew what they wanted. They were assumed, let us say, to be ready for practical teaching. While it would never have occurred to me that I was among this special section, and was fully prepared to go on patiently attending Ouspensky's evenings for instruction and preparation, I admit frankly that these evenings—yes—bored me. Much wisdom, I am sure, was sprayed over us, many valuable hints offered, practical as well as theoretical, but the net result when I made my way home, was negligible. To get a straight intelligible answer to a straight question was almost impossible. I listened attentively, but I never heard an intelligible—yes, an intelligent—question receive a satisfactory reply. The questioner was made to feel that his or her question was rather silly. No doubt the audience was mixed. The level of personal experience was often low. Theosophists, Spiritualists too, blared out half-digested questions about their particular dogmas and beliefs. They "asked for it", if we may put it so. But, at any rate, the replies did not favour further, brave questions. No help or guidance was vouchsafed. Sympathy, with a view to helping lame dogs over difficult stiles, was absent. With the result that questions became rarer and rarer. After a talk with Orage, I went straight to Ouspensky and asked if I could now go to Fontainebleau and, when he said "Yes", went off at once . . .

What I experienced at Fontainebleau does not belong to this brief word about Ouspensky. He remains a somewhat mythical figure. Of his intellectual and imaginative equipment there can be no question. The source of his "special inside knowledge", he has always admitted frankly, was his teacher, Gurdjieff. How he came across Gurdjieff I cannot be positive. The current story I heard everywhere was that when he went out East to examine for himself the lore of the so-called Eastern Wisdom, he ran into Gurdjieff in Constantinople—and suddenly realised he had met a man who knew it all and had been himself trained in some Occult School. And Gurdjieff, recognising a practical student who had already made certain progress working alone on his own lines, picked him out and gave him seven years special, intensified training. I repeat this for what it may be worth. I myself am sceptical as well as enquiring.

I stayed at the Fontainebleau establishment on several occasions, with repeated visits, and I heard there the vague story that the two men had disagreed in certain ways and that a separation had followed. Of that I cannot judge. Madame Ouspensky was still there and very much to the fore in the conduct of that extraordinary establishment. The preliminary training in yoga convinced me it was genuine and helpful for any serious student. The method of changing one's *type* of consciousness, rather than merely extending what one already possesses, seemed to me true and practical, for it was both severe and painful; moreover, it linked on intelligibly with what Ouspensky tried to give his listeners in the London meetings.

In my later visits there, when linguistic difficulties had become somewhat modified, I got the impression—though, please, very much for what it was worth—that Gurdjieff felt his old companion and disciple had given up his original severe self-training and slipped back into the easier trough of a mere "talker". That's as it may be; my "impression" may be quite unjustified. Once when I mentioned Ouspensky's name, Gurdjieff smiled and shrugged his shoulders: "Ouspensky," he commented, leaving it at that, "Ouspensky—a five dimensional man!" Not another word would he say. If not a sneer, it remains in my memory as a slight I rather resented.

At any rate, I am genuinely sorry that Ouspensky has left us; I owe him much. At the same time, it is to Gurdjieff that I owe most.

March 1948.

Notes

[1] There's a cluster of names in this first paragraph who need some introduction. Charles H. Hinton (1853-1907) was a mathematician and teacher who is best known for his treatise *Scientific Romances* (1884) which influenced H. G. Wells, and *A New Era of Thought* (1888) which fascinated Blackwood for its ideas on other dimensions. Ouspensky (1878-1947) was also inspired by Hinton especially for his first book *The Fourth Dimension* (1909), but his major work was *Tertium Organum* (1912), or the "Third Canon" following on from Aristotle and Francis Bacon. Ouspensky chose to turn everything on its head and challenge all existing ideas to see what alternatives might arise and fit within a great scheme. A copy of the book found its way to the USA where it was translated by architect Claude Bragdon (1866-1946) who was also interested in other dimensions and had already designed a hypercube. Georgi Gurdjieff (1866-1949) was a true mystic who believed humans existed in a kind of waking dream and that they

needed to push the body, physically and mentally in order to enter a higher state of conscious.

[2] Lady Rothermere (1875-1937) was the estranged wife of Lord Rothermere, publisher of the *Daily Mirror* and other newspapers. She had lost two of her sons during the war and was constantly seeking a form of restitution.

[3] Alfred Orage (1873-1934) was a socialist thinker and former schoolteacher who co-founded and became editor of *The New Age*, a socialist and political weekly which strove to modernise the pattern of thinking in the United Kingdom away from the Victorian era.

Adventures in Thought-Tranference

Two strange incidents, for which telepathy seems the only possible explanation, remain vividly in my memory, and are perhaps worth the telling. The first concerns a patient in a lunatic asylum whose violence was such that a strait-waistcoat and a padded cell were necessary. It came to my notice many years ago when I was a reporter on the *New York Sun*; it was of a private nature and had nothing to do with my reporting work; as all concerned have long since passed on, there is no possible objection to its being told.

Among my intimate friends in those New York days was an elderly lady of benevolent and philanthropic tendencies, whose sole object in life was to help others. She was a Swedenborgian, a faithful member of the New Church, and we discussed together the seer's philosophy of correspondences, his *Heaven and Hell*, and the rest, with some enthusiasm, although I never found myself particularly attracted to his particular angelic doctrines.

This lady's husband had been dead some years before I made her acquaintance, but I must mention his characteristics in passing. Chairman of a large provision business of some kind, he was a man of most exact and punctilious habits. Every detail of his daily life had to be precisely so. He never varied. From the choosing of a necktie to the hour of attendance at his office, he was as regular as clockwork. A most equable disposition into the bargain, never excited, never flurried. And a very wealthy man. Business was flourishing.

A time came, however, when apparently business ceased to be quite so flourishing, for, though he offered no explanation, a less luxurious scale of life became necessary. They moved into a smaller apartment. A few months later into a still smaller apartment and, so finally, into a really cheap flat. Money was obviously scarce; something was going badly in the business. Worse still, the husband's character began to show signs of the strain. For the first time in their happy married life, he began to betray irritability, unreasoning irritability.

At first it was hardly more than that, though now and again, she told me, she surprised expressions in his face and eyes that alarmed her. Whatever was troubling him—probably financial losses—he kept to himself. He had no outlet. It was all suppressed. In vain she provided openings. He kept it all hidden. The relief of expression, with its alleviation, possibly its cure, was denied to his cast-iron type. She watched it steadily grow worse, ignoring his outbursts of unreasonable temper—till, finally, there came a crack.

Unable to afford the expense of outside entertainment, they spent the evenings playing cards together—when she prayed he might win, since by this time losing infuriated him. But one evening, it seems, she could not help winning; so she cheated, but not cleverly enough. He caught her at it. His face was aflame as he sprang to his feet, took her by the throat and said he was going to kill her.

This rather wonderful woman played the right card. Without a struggle, she offered him her throat, with the remark that she wanted to die. His hands dropped, the violence left him, he collapsed, almost in tears. It is unnecessary to tell in detail how, surreptitiously, she persuaded a famous alienist to examine him, with the latter's grave warning that her life was in danger and that her husband must be certified insane. She must never be alone with him . . . so that, in due course, he was removed to the Bloomingdale Asylum for the Insane, where she went every day to visit him. He never once recognised her; nor, such was his violent condition, could she ever go into his presence in the padded cell without either the doctor or an attendant.

It is here that the "strange incident" comes in, the incident which seems to offer only telepathy as an explanation.

By his first marriage, the patient had a son to whom he was devoted; and this son, being in a distant land, could not, of course, go to see his afflicted father. Let us call him John. And one unforgettable morning, as my friend took the tram on her daily visit to the Asylum, she read in the newspaper that John had met with an accident and been killed. She decided, of course, that it was better to say nothing about it to her husband. In the first place, he never recognised her, usually mistaking her for the cook or servant in their flat; and for the second, the shock might prove too serious for him. She asked the doctor, however, whether her husband ever saw a newspaper and was somewhat relieved to hear that he never asked for one and never saw one.

"But," added the doctor, "you will be glad to know that today, ever since yesterday afternoon in fact, your husband has been enjoying a lucid interval. I will come into the cell with you, but I think this time he will recognise you and know who you are. He's been as gentle as a lamb."

And such proved to be the case. The patient came up to her, embraced her affectionately, knew who she was—then asked: "But tell me, please. What's happened to John? Is John all right? Is he really dead as he told me yesterday?"

The shock of, first the complete recognition, then of the question, she somehow contrived to manage without a direct answer. The sympathetic and understanding doctor helped her. Goodbye till tomorrow was said happily enough, though the patient was clearly not fully satisfied.

On the way out the doctor learned the facts of the son's death from her. "That's very strange," he said; "yesterday afternoon your husband sent for me. He was calm and lucid, but he was deeply worried about something. He kept asking me if his son, John, was all right. John, he kept repeating, had spoken to him audibly, saying he had just been killed in an accident."

A day or two later the mania became intensified and the patient ended his life with a stroke.

The other "strange incident" is of a more directly personal kind. It took place in London.

The lady I have already mentioned came over on a visit and I often went to her hotel to see her. Again, we talked about Swedenborg and his philosophy, but we also discussed her strong belief that the spirit leaves the body in sleep, and that although the memory of its experiences out of the body may only rarely be recoverable next day, such experiences have value. We decided on making the experiment together and to see (a) if we could meet out of the body, (b) if we could bring back any memory of such meeting.

"Just before going to sleep," she said, "register the wish, the determination rather, to meet. Do this quietly but with conviction. Do not stress it unduly, because that may stir opposition or criticism. Merely tell yourself that we *are* going to meet out of the body, and leave it at that."

I agreed to do this and went home fully prepared to carry out faithfully my part of the bargain. On reaching my rooms in Chelsea, however, I found a letter that greatly disturbed me. It was from a sister who was in grave trouble, asking my advice and help; and this letter took complete possession of my mind and thoughts. It had to be answered immediately for delivery by the first post next morning, but my reply involved care and long consideration. In due course it was written and I went out to post it—and so eventually to bed. All memory of our proposed experiment, however, had by then completely left my mind. It was utterly forgotten. And no dreams came to trouble my sleep.

It was the following day when I went to my friend's hotel to tea that the memory came back, and I found myself obliged to explain how it was I had forgotten to carry out my side of the bargain.

My friend, however, forestalled me: "Let me tell you my story first," she said, "and then you can tell me yours."

And this is what she told me.

"Before going to sleep," she said, "I quietly registered the desire that we might meet out of the body, and then dropped off. During the night I had a vivid dream in which I was searching and searching to find you, but was always blocked by something that kept persistently in front of me barring my way. It was something big and dark obstructing my way, something I could not pass, try as I would. I cannot say it was a figure exactly, because I could not determine a definite outline. It just stopped my advancing so that I could not pass. I remember then making a tremendous effort to force my way through and past it, when a voice came from it. And this voice, quite clear and definite, said: 'There is no use trying to find A. because he is with his sister.' "

These instances, which suggest a telepathic explanation, bring to mind another curious case that may be worth the telling, although it has no obvious relation with telepathy. Its explanation, indeed, is hard to find. It is sufficiently singular to have remained vividly in my memory over a number of years; and, though being abroad at the time and was unable to investigate it at first hand, it was told to me by persons whom I regard as worthy of belief.

It is the story of a man who was haunted by a face—a terrifying, horrific, demonic face. It came and went, apparently, as it pleased, nor could he relate to it anything he had ever read or thought or dreamed. It would appear at the most inopportune moments, peering at him over his shoulder when he was dressing or shaving, reflected in the looking-glass, thrusting itself forward when he was with friends, when he was driving his car, walking along the street on his lawful occasions, or sitting down at home reading a book. Its visits seemed to have no meaning, least of all as a warning of some imminent disaster. Its origin entirely escaped him. Though a human face it was diabolical. It terrified him. His nerves went to pieces. He consulted clergymen, psychiatrists, healers, all in vain. The awful face kept at him. As a professional man, his work suffered; his health too. According to the story told to me, his trouble reached the ears of a young doctor, more open-minded than most of his profession, who managed to get into touch with him and suggested an experiment he thought might effect a cure. He invited the man to his country cottage for a week-end, discussing his affliction with sympathy and understanding, winning his confidence and co-operation.

"I propose to photograph the face," he explained. "I'll have my camera always ready. Let's keep in contact day and night. Make me a sign when the face appears and I'll take a photograph of it. If nothing appears on the plate, we shall at least know that it's subjective—evoked by something in your own mind. Once we know that, we can try to trace its origin. You agree? Good."

It was on the Sunday morning, as they sat reading the papers in deck chairs on the lawn, that a frightened cry, "Here it is! Over my left shoulder" brought the doctor's camera instantly into action.

"You got it," cried the man, as the camera clicked. "You got us both! It turned its eyes toward you as the snap came." He was shaking with terror. The doctor had seen nothing except his patient's chalk-white face. He hurried off to develop the negative. But it was a long time before he re-emerged to announce the result, much longer than was necessary to obtain a proof, and his explanation of the delay was obviously lame and unconvincing. The photograph was a failure. The lens had been directed into the sun. There hadn't been time to point it properly. They must try again . . . The young doctor was perturbed, though he tried to conceal something that had evidently shocked him. No second chance of taking a photograph occurred. The haunted man never learned what had actually appeared on the plate.

Such was the story as it was given me. I told it briefly in a broadcast with several other strange incidents that seemed to me interesting. Among the letters that reached me from listeners was the following:

"The story which interested me most in your recent broadcast was the one about the man who saw a face over his shoulder. In the capacity of spiritual healer I was asked to visit a man living somewhere in the south counties. I stayed with him and his wife several times and did what I could to free him from his horrible obsession, without— apparently—any success. Once he drove me up to London in his car and it was quite the most nerve-wracking experience I have ever been through, because he drove like a veritable Jehu, and kept turning his head to look at the horrible face which he said was constantly haunting him. How we escaped a smash I can never understand, but we did manage to arrive safely in London. He was a successful member of a well-known profession, and I should so like to know if your man could possibly be the same. If so, your photographic sequel would prove very interesting and would explain much at which I only guessed. As a matter of fact I did try exorcism, but he was a difficult subject and I felt that I had failed completely."

December 1949.

Notes

[1] The lady in the first two anecdotes was Virginia Kent (1842-1930). She had been married to George Lewis Kent (1827-1884) who had established a profitable business in the grocery trade. His son from an earlier marriage, Frederick Cleaveland Kent, had committed suicide on 10 December 1884 and his father's death came just two weeks later, on 22 December, as Blackwood recalled. Blackwood is unlikely to have known her much before late 1893.

[2] I have not been able to find any details about the man haunted by the face, nor do I know the identity of the doctor who took the photograph. Blackwood's own doctor, Vincent Nesfield (1879-1962) was interested in this type of phenomena and, had he taken the photo, he would certainly have told Blackwood what he'd seen on the plate.

Oddities

I wonder if you have got what I call a favourite adjective—not such a silly question as it sounds perhaps—an adjective you can always fall back upon in time of trouble, one you may be inclined to overwork, rather? Not so long ago, you may remember, it was "wizard", everything was qualified as "wizard". But that has faded away, thank heaven. And I am asking my question because I have got a favourite one of my own which I find uncommonly useful in ordinary social intercourse: the adjective "odd".

I am interested in the strange things of life, and people often tell me their strange experiences, or—the other way round—I tell my own. For strange experiences seem to insist on being shared, a measure of guarantee, perhaps, against the fear of being thought a bit crazy? Maybe! And this is where my favourite little adjective comes in so useful. A friend, for instance, tells me something it is rather hard to believe; and, wondering if he is pulling my leg, out trots my adjective: "Yes—er—that's very odd!" Or, *vice versa*, I am tempted to tell some queer experience of my own: "Heavens!" he exclaims, disbelief all over his face. "By Jove, yes . . . that's mighty odd—isn't it?" "Odd" is the right adjective often enough, though it is a cowardly one. It hedges. Anyhow, it leaves the door open for a more definite comment later on if called for. And it is more polite than a blunt "Nonsense! I don't believe you!"

Here is an instance of the type of strange experience that deserved that little adjective I find so useful. It has happened to me rarely, I admit, just now and again, but it has happened . . . happened, too, to many other people if reports be true. I am walking along a crowded London street, my mind packed with the nonsense of the day, when I suddenly see Smith some twenty yards ahead, and coming towards me. Unless I shoot across the road we are bound to meet. Now, I haven't seen Smith for weeks or months, nor thought about him. He means nothing to me specially, just a pleasant acquaintance. I quickly give him a second look. It is, unquestionably, Smith. A few yards later, a couple of minutes or so, we meet. It is *not* Smith. Nor has the stranger any particular resemblance to Smith. You have guessed what's coming, no doubt; for, later in the day, barging along another crowded street elsewhere in London town, I run bang into the real Smith. Isn't that a bit odd? What on earth brought the fellow so vividly into my mind that I plastered his face on someone else and imagined I actually saw him? Once, when I asked this alleged Smith whether he had been thinking of me lately at all, the answer was unflattering: "No—er—can't say I have", or something similar.

A common explanation of this strange occurrence some think is telepathy. Maybe . . . ! We need not go into the wearisome technique of that theory, but an interesting point perhaps is that what is called "delayed telepathy" has its supporters. For, assuming that a strong thought-impulse from a distant friend does reach me, it does not follow that it registers immediately in my conscious mind. For this conscious mind may be so bogged up with the clamorous details of the actual moment that it cannot get through. It lies waiting in some suburban region till it finds an opening. In any case, the qualifying adjective is "odd".

Having got rid of Smith and his somewhat vulnerable appearance, may I risk telling you another personal experience?

[...]

Some twenty-five years ago, while writing *The Education of Uncle Paul* [1909], I was living in a village in the Jura Mountains above Neuchâtel, and it was my habit to spend the entire day with a notebook wandering over the hills and forests. The notebook, often containing a whole chapter, was very precious to me.

One evening, on getting back late from a day's wandering, the book was missing. It was neither in my pocket nor my knapsack. I had lost it. The loss, naturally, worried me very much. Having covered many miles of hill and forest during the long summer's day, it seemed hopeless to go out next day and search. I could not even remember exactly what my route had been.

I was very tired and slept deeply, but during the night I was once—for a second or two merely—just aware of turning over in bed. It was no more than that—the consciousness that my body turned from one side to the other, for I certainly did not wake. In that brief second, however, I saw something. I saw a shallow rivulet of clear running water that danced and rippled in the sunshine and just beneath the surface lay the outline of my black notebook. I saw it very distinctly, its outline wavering a little as the ripples ran over it. It lay in about two inches of water. I saw the white limestone pebbles on which is rested.

Properly speaking, this was not a dream, for there was no sequence of events, and nothing happened. The next second I was in deep sleep again.

In the morning, luckily, I recalled this vivid picture. I also, after some reflection, recalled having knelt down to drink from a tiny rivulet. Though uncertain as to its exact whereabouts, I thought I might find the spot, and I set out for the tramp of many hours again. I did find it. I found my notebook, too, precisely as the picture of the night had shown it to me. It lay there, under some two inches of clear water with bright sunlight gleaming on it. My pencil notes, too, were quite legible.

The explanation here, of course, is simple: it had slipped from pocket or knapsack as I knelt to drink. And I had seen it slip out, though my consciousness, concentrated on my eager thirst, had not noticed it. During sleep my subconscious merely brought the picture back.[1]

[. . .]

"Odd", yes, oh, distinctly "odd". Isn't it a grand and useful adjective? I really could not get through the day's routine without it, let alone the awful post-bag. So may I bring back our old friend Smith, for a moment? And this "odd" occurrence has, apparently, poked its nose up so frequently that even the Psychical Research Society has looked into it, and its theme has crept into fiction. And it runs, more or less, along familiar lines like this: Smith dreams repeatedly of a house or garden or landscape—then suddenly comes across it in the lawful occasions of his daily life. He recognises it in detail, knowing precisely where that path leads to or what lies in the next room when he opens the door. He has been here so often in his recurrent dream that he cannot be mistaken. Nor, indeed, is he mistaken. And so it runs along the familiar lines, as you possibly have heard, till the caretaker, or someone in charge of the place admits, in answer to a tactful question: "Yes, sir, the house is said to be haunted; but you, sir, are the ghost. I've seen you here myself, more than once."

And here is another, final incident—a true one—entitled to my favourite adjective. I merely report it as it happened. A young married friend in the R.A.F. during the war, went into the travel business and had the luck to find a flat in Hampstead. A telephone was of primary importance to him. It was hard to get. He went through the usual delays and difficulties, all understandable and reasonable enough. The G.P.O. was helpful and sympathetic. But the long delay hampered his business.

One night he had a dream, brief and of no interest. Merely that he was fixing up a ticket abroad for somebody—a stranger—and the prospective client asked for his address. He gave it. "And your telephone number?" asked the client. In reply to which normal enquiry, and without an instant's hesitation, my friend gave it: "Hampstead – – – – " and four numbers. And then woke up.

It so happened that my friend was interested in the theories about time and precognition (seeing the future in dreams) and took the trouble to note down the telephone number he had so glibly given in his dream, just on the off-chance, as it were. His wife also wrote it down. A few days later he told me the dream too and asked me to write the number down. We all did this. Time passed. We forgot all about this number, but at least it was honestly recorded by the three of us. We had it accurately in writing. The permutations of four numbers run, of course, into fantastic possibilities.[2]

Some six weeks later my friend's telephone was duly installed. He got his number—it was the number he had given in his dream . . . "Very odd, yes," said people to whom I reported these facts. Personally, however, I hardly think it necessary to claim precognition as the explanation.

That number, before it was finally allocated, was known to several workers in the telephone service. Thus our old friend telepathy, universal aunt of psychical research, though equally wonderful, seems an explanation. The exchange, moreover, was not Hampstead, but Primrose—a minor slip, perhaps.

31 August 1948.

Notes

[1] Blackwood repeated here the anecdote about Mrs. Kent's attempts to contact him in her dreams, which can be found in "Adventures in Thought-Transference". Rather than duplicate it, I have deleted that section and replaced it with a contribution he made to the symposium "Some Remarkable Dreams" for *The Strand Magazine* (February 1933).

[2] The "friend" was actually Blackwood's nephew Patrick (1912-1975) who had served in the RAF in India.

Gooseflesh

The following was an interview conducted with Blackwood as part of the radio series Books and Authors.

BBC: *When writing one of your really creepy stories do you, yourself, get a feeling of this so-called "gooseflesh", or a chill down the spine?*

AB: If I didn't feel it myself, it doesn't get across. Actually, in fact, it's feeling the creeps or gooseflesh that starts the story. No creepy story starts without that first shock of the uncanny. Once felt, your instinct—if you're a writer—is obviously to give expression to your emotion in a story. Oddly enough, an emotion tries to express itself—to *dramatise* itself— hence the story. Without that first stimulating thrill, any story remains still-born. No story results. But—and this is a big but—I must obviously be thrilled myself—feel that chill down the spine—before I can hope to "get it across", in story form. Interesting, perhaps, to remember the primitive origin of this gooseflesh. An animal, when frightened, wants to make itself as big and fierce-looking as it can. Up goes its fur, its hackles. Well, our hair or fur has gone, but the action of the pores or hair roots remains.

BBC: *I'd never heard that before. But tell me, where do you get it from, this shock of something unusual, uncanny, other-*

worldly, call it what you will. What is its origin? What causes it in your own case, for instance?

AB: Your question is good and penetrating. I'd love to answer it. You want to know in terms of the man in the street, let us say, what starts this shock of the queer, the uncanny, the so-called supernatural sensation. Where, for instance, do I myself get it from. In a few words, it's hard to summarise, but it comes, I think, from the usual appearing suddenly *unusual*. A normal incident in normal life— catching a bus, meeting a friend, anything—suddenly and, above all, *inexplicably*, takes on another guise. You are puzzled, worried, even scared a bit. The incident is over. What's the explanation? You don't know. "That's odd," you say to yourself, and you feel an unpleasant thrill down the spine—gooseflesh.

BBC: *That may be, but, after all, it doesn't get much further.*

AB: Agreed. One further answer, I think, is that anything "out of the ordinary" alarms us. Most of us are mere mechanical automata. The machine then plays tricks—and we are suddenly scared to death.

BBC: *But what gives you, personally, gooseflesh?*

AB: Well, I think my best answer is that it's something, some incident, some combination of atmosphere and accidental surroundings at a given moment—anywhere— at home, in a forest, on a lonely mountain, out in the desert, on the tube—suddenly seems *unnatural*, and therefore inexplicable. And it *frightens*.

BBC: *But why? Why the chill down the spine?*

AB: Because, firstly, it's unusual. Secondly, and I believe this is vital, because it stirs to life in me a touch of those old primitive instincts of long ago. The fear of the dark, the dread of the external animistic universe, when a clap of thunder was a god roaring. This underbed of superstitious terror lies in every one of us. It is still easily evoked. The unusual, the inexplicable, awakens it. This deep thrill of superstition in us—above all in our so-called intellectuals, who are both ashamed to admit it and puzzled to explain it—is still active subconsciously. Humanity still lies rather terrifyingly close to the primitive caveman, with his fear of the dark.

BBC: *You mention superstition—do you mean in a derogatory sense?*

AB: On the contrary. Superstition lies more or less hidden in all of us and is too easily tapped in daily life. We all recognise that. The so-called supernatural is a different question. It's a silly, meaningless phrase. Everything is natural and under natural laws. Only there are other laws of which we are so far ignorant.

BBC: *Such as . . . ?*

AB: An aboriginal, hearing my voice suddenly out of a box is pure magic, because he is ignorant of the natural laws producing it.

BBC: *Coming back to our subject . . .*

AB: Quite so—and why it's been the theme of so many of my stories, *John Silence* among them. Well, I imagine the vein of primitive superstition lives on in me. I love a ghost story. As a boy, my father told me lovely ones, though he, being evangelical, attributed them mostly to a personal devil. Then I went searching for myself and found others. Few had the authentic touch, I'm afraid. Few gave me the real genuine gooseflesh we're talking about. The clever ones were invented by the brain, the mind, admirable in their construction and literary craft, but—and it's a big "but"—the writers hadn't felt in themselves that awful otherworldly thrill of personal experience. I find it rarely, this awful personal thrill. How well I remember, be the result good or bad, feeling so frightened while writing that I had to sit with my chair against the wall—with the horrible feeling that something might get at me from behind while I was writing, in an Alpine hut . . .

BBC: *What story was that?*

AB: "The Wendigo" . . . it scared me stiff. I well remember being afraid to go to sleep without the light on.

BBC: *And other writers?*

AB: I devour everything in the field, but the authentic touch is rare. The brain doesn't write "gooseflesh" tales. The frightened heart does.[1]

BBC: *Thank you, Mr. Blackwood.*

31 January 1948.

Notes

[1] In a letter to August Derleth dated 10 June 1946, Blackwood noted that authors whom he felt never failed to please included A. E. Coppard, Mary Wilkins Freeman, May Sinclair, H. Russell Wakefield, and Henry S. Whitehead. He also singled out Henry James's *The Turn of the Screw* (1898) as bringing a "sense of wonder" to the thrill of horror.

Along Came a Spider

I share our lovely green planet with another inhabitant who inspires me with a degree of loathing that includes fear, even horror. If brought suddenly face to face with this repulsive individual, something akin to paralysis attacks my muscular system so that for a passing moment I seem unable to act. I stand and stare, fascinated, frightened, without knowing why.

You've guessed, of course. I'm talking of my private, personal phobia: a spider. Now, phobias are very common, especially this one of spiders; and a phobia is a secret fear for which no explanation occurs. The pre-natal theory is discarded, auto-suggestion doesn't work, it is a groundless yet persistent fear, innate, in the blood. It appears often in the most fantastic forms, but while you can laugh at the fluttering moths that terrify some people, you never can laugh at your own. Spiders are *not* ludicrous to myself.

I dislike their nasty hairy legs, their two greedy swollen abdomens, their vile way of eating their bound and helpless prey or, when bigger, snatching tiny birds from the nest before they can fly. Their eight eyes, too, are sinister, since you can't know what they're really looking at, or what kind of portrait they see. Horrible, too, is the way the female devours her husband even before she's divorced him.

All these, however, are surface blemishes; there is something much deeper than all that—if—if I could only get at it. Does a big spider, for instance, radiate something inimical in the way some folk think a cat announces its near presence long before it is seen? The mere idea is comic, yet, if I see a big spider on the ceiling of my bedroom, I can't go to sleep until I have persuaded the monster to leave.

Naturally, friends declare that a fright in early childhood explains my phobia, though it is wholly untrue. Yet I recall a recurrent nightmare in childhood and youth that haunted me, but it was an after-effect rather than a cause.

In my sleep I first heard something creeping cautiously across the carpet towards my bed. On reaching the sheets it began to climb stealthily. With its fantastic eyes it picked out available hand-or-foot holds. Once on the counterpane I could hear its nasty scrabbling feet as it crawled along the edge of the sheets and blankets where these lay against my cheeks. And then it paused, eyeing me no doubt from fantastic angles with its horrible, queer eyes. A feathery touch brushed my skin. I woke—or thought I woke in the nightmare—and there, staring at me, perched a big, dark spider.

The nightmare broke. I shot out of bed. No sign of a spider anywhere. Had it been a fly, a beetle, a caterpillar, I wouldn't have cared tuppence. The horror of the nightmare clung for some minutes. But, anyhow, this nightmare was not the *cause* of my phobia.

I've often asked myself why this beast is so repulsive and frightening to people like myself with a form of spider phobia, but no cure resulted. They often have lovely covering. Also no teeth to bite you, and very few carry poison glands. Its legs may be unpleasant to look at, I know, yet it is provided with an ingenious contrivance that constructs faultlessly the geometrical wonder of their web. With the morning dew sparkling on that taut, elastic structure, few sights are more lovely. The tiny kind that adventure gaily for great distances on barely visible strips of gossamer contribute an authentic touch of fairyland. I stand with hat off in admiration and respect to their amazing skill and ingenuity from the trap-door spider onwards.

Thus, I have tried to see both sides of the horror, as it were; my hate is not just blind hate. Moreover, spiders possess yet another distinction I'm sure they are proud of: they are not insects, because they have eight legs instead of six. They have their own family name which they share with scorpions—*Arachnidae*. So, there it is! The more I study them, the less can I understand why this acute form of phobia can remain in my blood all these years of my long life. Nor has any doctor I have asked given me any clue.

I recall an unpleasant incident with a tarantula once— in Toronto, where long ago I shared a ground floor in a boarding house with another English boy. Folding doors divided us. One afternoon he greeted me with an expression of rapture: "Oh, I say, what d'you think I've got?" With immense pride he opened a small box he held. I saw inside a full-size, hairy-legged tarantula. Big as a mouse! He had bought a bunch of bananas from some southern state. The tarantula was a stowaway. I watched him stroke the devil— yes, actually *stroke* it. I saw the pride and happiness in his eyes. He was seventeen. I was over eighteen.[1]

I concealed my ludicrous phobia. He couldn't detect my icy shudder. I begged him to be careful. "It's dangerously poisonous," I mentioned, "but won't attack unless frightened." Oh yes, he knew all that. I went out while he kept repeating, "Isn't it a beauty . . . " An hour or two later I came in to bed. He greeted me. "Oh I say—it's escaped!" A search of the two dingy rooms, with so many dark corners, was a waste of time. I went to bed.

When I opened my eyes in the morning I saw the monster stuck to the wall facing me across the small bedroom. It was close to a hot-air pipe in the wall. Adrenalin poured into my blood, but I knew enough not to attack. If left alone it would merely watch me out of its fantastic eyes, all its horrid legs ready to leap, but otherwise quiet. How I wriggled out of bed and crawled inch by inch, covered by sheets and blankets lest even a toe might stick out, and reached the door, I leave to the imagination. At the door, however, I was compelled to stretch out an uncovered arm to turn the handle. Once safely in the passage I turned— the monster, of course, hadn't moved. My young friend later picked it off with his ungloved fingers.

It is not always easy to establish what is, or is not, a genuine phobia, but at any rate the obvious fears—tigers, poisonous snakes, fire—common to all of us, conceal no secret cause. Is, for instance, a bat in the phobia class? Some people whom I've asked if they have a phobia that haunts them say, at once, "Oh yes, bats of course! I'm terrified of bats!" A bat, we know, may especially alarm women when it darts by chance through an open window into the room, but that's no mystery, because they fear it may get entangled in their long hair. The wonderful radar wings make such a disaster extremely unlikely, for every object in the room sends its message instantly and the bat immediately avoids striking it. The long hair is quite safe. If the lights are turned on, since bright light distresses it, the bat will dart out again into the dusk where its food is waiting in a moment or two. They are mysterious creatures, none the less, possessed of unusual powers.

Now, what of the large blood-sucking vampires. These have been carefully studied in Bolivia where their feeding habits do great harm to cattle in the fields at night. And a particular group of scientists established that a vampire would never touch a human being before he was genuinely asleep—and no pretence of being asleep could deceive them. The men under their blankets might snore, lie motionless, breathe deeply and assume all the posture of profound slumber, but no bat would come near them. Sooner or later, of course, they would slip off into genuine slumber—and in flitted the bat noiselessly, having spotted a toe or finger not under cover, and next morning they'd've lost a quantity of blood. Moreover, this creature's very sharp incisor teeth have been thoughtfully equipped by nature with a minute gland of some kind that injects a drop of some soothing mixture so that the pain of the prick is not even felt. The man slumbers on undisturbed.

Anyhow, I don't think bats or cats can be regarded as genuine phobias that exercise their strange gifts on us by way of foolish and quite unnecessary terrors.

A remarkable case of a woman's acute spider-phobia crops up: apparently she knew a big spider was in her room before she saw it. I read this case in a medical journal of repute, though without editorial sanction. It was either an article or a letter. Her own spider phobia was too acute to be laughed away; her temperature went up, there were genuine hysterics, even the heart was affected. Her husband, who treated these outbursts with sympathy and understanding, heard her scream for help one afternoon and dashed up to her bedroom when she had gone to rest.

"A big spider is in the room," she cried. "I haven't seen it. For goodness sake get it out . . . "

She was in acute distress. He searched in vain, soothing her as best he could. Presently his brother joined in the search and later, quite by chance, his eye picked out a large garden spider lying among the toilet articles on the dressing-table, cleverly camouflaged by chance. Without saying a word he quietly squashed it. The woman on the sofa at the end of the room could not possibly have seen this, but instantly cried out in a voice of intense relief, "Oh, it's gone!" She soon recovered her equanimity.

Now I know that many haters of cats claim to know if there's one about long before they see it. A cat, an electrical beastie but a great pal of mine, may conceivably radiate a warning message, but I find it hard to believe that a spider has any gift of that sort. But who knows? I certainly do not.

While chatting about these falsely called "insects", an incident comes to mind where a woman with a real spider phobia, though not acute, paid a morning visit to her garden in the sunshine and chatted with her gardener. A huge garden spider flaunted its wonder in the centre of its beautiful web beside her. She made some unkind remark the gardener was accustomed to. "They're not bad to eat, you know, madam," he observed, as he picked it out of the web, gave a quick chew, and swallowed it. "A bit on the sweet side, I always think," he added, selecting another even fatter and juicier.

Among the creepy-crawlies, though only spiders bring horror, I had an adventure in Egypt with a scorpion. Apart from the normal fear of its nasty sting, I have nothing against it. But one morning, getting ready for a long walk in the desert, I pulled on my big walking boots and felt something wriggling under my foot. A scorpion . . . ?

What to do? The instant the pressure of my foot, snugly inside, was lifted, up would come the tail and I'd get stung. How could I loosen the boot and get my foot out without that tail shooting up and injecting its nasty poison? That was the problem. I got the laces out, but didn't dare raise my foot. It would be too quick for me. I had my knife out, ready to slit the expensive leather and ruin the boot. I remembered the legend that a scorpion surrounded by fire will commit suicide by stinging itself, but I knew that was fake. The heat merely contracts the tail muscles and up goes the sting. I began to despise that scorpion in my precious boot.

After a deep breath, I drew out my foot, and saw the innocent little baby locust half squashed but still full of life . . . ! I enjoyed my walk.[2]

10 June 1950.

Notes

[1] Blackwood arrived in Toronto in May 1890 when he was already twenty-one, so it's odd he would seem to suggest he was younger. I do not know the identity of the boy he shared lodgings with. His closest friend in Toronto was Johann Pauw, English of Dutch descent, but he was nearly three years older.

[2] Curiously Blackwood fails to mention his story "An Egyptian Hornet", included in *Day and Night Stories* (1917), which may have been inspired by the locust incident, but where the narrator has a phobia for a hornet which invades his bathroom.

The Fear of Heights

A re you, perhaps, one of many people who can't stand heights—what's usually called a bad or a good head? I mean, could you lean out of a fortieth storey window in a New York skyscraper without a shudder. Or look over the edge of an Alpine precipice into several thousand feet of empty space without that quivering flutter in your solar plexus the airmen called "butterflies in the tummy"?

This fear-of-heights business has always interested me. It puzzles me. My type of mind likes to get things explained, but I've never found a satisfying explanation of why some people shudder and turn a little sick and why others are absolutely immune.

Climbing, especially rock, as against ice climbing, is a hobby of mine. I've come across many instances of people who are terrified, and of people who are completely immune. On occasions I've experienced the terror myself, so I know what I'm talking about. In what are called "exposed" positions—clambering up a sheer rock-face with precarious foot holds above a yawning drop—I've felt it: though never severely enough to make me an unsafe companion on the rope. It has the strange quality of nightmare terror, and I know of nothing comparable to that—when even after waking you're afraid to go to sleep again lest it return.

It is no ordinary fear, and the fear of falling doesn't quite account for it, though it may contribute. It's something more than that. Nor has it anything to do with so-called Mountain Sickness, due largely to a lack of oxygen at a certain height above sea-level. No, it's something different. Its symptoms are a weakening of legs and knees, a sudden distrust of foot- and hand-folds, a feeling that your nailed boots are so huge you're bound to stumble over the next step, in fact a lack of co-ordination between brain and muscles. There's no actual giddiness, oddly enough, though it's wiser not to look down where the cows are the size of rabbits and the fir trees look like ferns. Anyhow, though I've experienced these awful moments, I've never had to ask my companions to blindfold me. [1]

A memory of that connection comes back to me. We are three on a rope going with extreme caution down an "exposed" position when one of us, a most experienced climber, announced quietly, "I've got an attack coming on; better blindfold me." It was a courageous thing to say, from a man who actually was our leader. He knew that if he slipped we never could have held him. There were no delays possible. We should have plunged, all three, into several thousand feet of empty space—towards those tiny cows and trees like ferns. Luckily it was a short pitch. We blindfolded him, putting his feet carefully in the correct holds, his hands likewise. No unnecessary word was spoken. We moved one at a time. Oddly enough his admission of weakness increased my own not over-strong sense of security.

This reminds me of a case of complete immunity though it provides me with a moment of nightmare shudder. Climbing once with a Swiss guide and two friends, we were lunching on a wide, safe ledge, our legs hanging over a drop of many thousand feet. The rope was off. We were enjoying ourselves. The ledge, dead level and not sloping outwards was, perhaps, six feet. We got talking about this fear of heights business and the guide just couldn't understand it. He asked for an explanation. Why did people feel giddy and so forth? No satisfactory explanation was forthcoming. Then he suddenly proceeded to stand on his head, balancing on his hands, laughing at us from his up-turned face. "You see," he said, "there's no danger. In your bedroom you'd do it easily!" It gave me a true nightmare squirm to watch him.

Many years ago I watched a man walk across Niagara on what is called a tight-rope. He was a photographer in Toronto, Dixon by name. I knew him well. The tight-rope actually was the one Blondin had used many years earlier, just below the falls and before the rapids begin. It was still in place, a cable of sorts, thick as my arm. I was one of some forty thousand people who came that broiling summer day to watch. No charge was made. It was a free show. Dixon thought the publicity would be good for his business. We watched in breathless silence as he went, step by step, across above the racing river below, a drop of some 160 feet. He used an immense balancing pole. He never faltered. He lay down on his back half way across. Even up the steep inclines on either side, where the cable was fastened to the cliff edge, he moved confidently. I was running a small hotel in Toronto at the time. I asked him to lunch and questioned him.

"Safe as a house," he told me, "provided you move slowly and steadily in a certain rhythm. I have no fear of heights anyway. If that cable was only three or four feet above the ground anybody could walk, even run, along it in perfect safety. But one thing," he emphasised, "I never once looked down. That racing water below me was better not seen. It might have confused my sight a bit. If I had lost balance and fallen into those tearing rapids I wouldn't have had a dog's chance. And," he added, "I never understood how Captain Webb believed he could swim across where he tried."[2]

I asked him about the fear of heights so many people have. He had no explanation. "I guess it's mostly imagination," he suggested. Possibly a clue lies there . . . for artists, being imaginative folk, I've found, are usually afraid of dizzy ledges and sheer drops. Yet personally I feel that all generalisations, including this one, are dangerous. I remember also asking him his ideas about people who feel the irresistible impulse to throw themselves down from a height. His answer has at least a touch of plausibility. "I guess," he said, "they just can't stand the strain. They want to get it over—and jump." But here, again, generalisations are dangerous.

To return to this unexplained terror of heights—is there a cure? My enquiries have brought no satisfactory answer. Could suggestion under hypnosis, or even autosuggestion, get rid of it? I'm not sure that the former has even been tried. People who haven't got a good head don't bother about it. Why should they? They just keep away from dizzy mountain edges and book a room on the ground floor of a sky-scraper. I have talked with many doctors. Some say it is due to the mysterious channel behind the ear which, in sinus or other trouble, affects the sense of balance. Others say frankly they don't know, but incline to the idea that people who fear heights are also sufferers from sea-sickness. Facts hardly support the theory. Yet, I recall the case of a famous climber, to whom fear of heights was unknown, feeling so giddy in the captive balloon which went up a mere thousand feet from the Parc Monceau in Paris before the War, that he had to lie flat in the basket, while women looked gaily over the edge, because he just couldn't stand it. He collapsed, much to his shame. He said that if his eye hadn't followed the attaching cable to the ground he would have felt nothing. In his case sight obviously seemed the cause of his overmastering giddiness.

And it is a curious fact that people who fear heights feel nothing in an aeroplane. They look over the edge at any height without the slightest tremor of alarm. Would they feel frightened if they saw a cable attaching the plane to the ground?

The fear of slipping, of an actual fall, seems to have little to do with this mysterious terror. If the risk on some exposed position is serious, it only means taking extra care. And there's some interesting evidence about actual falling with its sensations. I recall a curious account by a very experienced climber who seems to have had every possible kind of climbing accident yet to have survived them all. He declared that the worst moment of all is when you feel the slip is coming, or *may* be coming. Your foothold under your nailed boot moves. You are no longer secure. It is a matter of seconds only, even of split seconds, but he describes this very brief moment as horrifying in the extreme. It's an agony. What follows, when the slide down has started, involves neither pain nor terror.

He experienced this on one occasion when, climbing alone, he was crossing the head of an extremely steep gully that plunged down hundreds of feet to a snow-field far below. He was using the utmost care when he felt his precarious foothold moving. He was unable to improve it. The slip was coming. He couldn't check it. It came. Those few seconds, he says, were agonising. But once he had started downwards, at first slowly, then with increasing speed, all fear left him. He tried to brake with his ice-axe before it was wrenched from his grasp and went spinning into space below him. He followed it. There was nothing he could do about it. But he kept his wits about him as he shot down, keenly observant all the time. The gully was narrowly enclosed between the cliffs on either side and he banged from one rock wall to the other like any falling stone. The concussion of each impact must have been very severe, yet he was hardly aware of each shock as it came, and his powers of observation never left him. He even tried to estimate where precisely the next crash would come so that he could meet it with his side or shoulder instead of with his head—for that would have been the end. And when the impact came, he felt no pain. Fear, too, was wholly absent. His consciousness was vivid and alert all the time, almost in some odd way intensified. And he used a strange word to describe what happened to his body: electrisation. He was aware of some kind of electrisation—whatever he meant by that. He did not lose consciousness when, finally, he landed in the snow-field and, after a long rest, continued his journey to the hut.

It seems queer to me, too, that this fear of heights is absent in sleep and dreams. Somnambulists, for instance, seem free of it. Authentic cases have been observed where the sleepwalker, afraid of heights in their waking state, is seen walking in perfect safety along the edge of a wall or roof with a nasty drop below. Provided he is not wakened he is in no danger. And in this connection I've read the suggestive explanation—with what proof I cannot say—that in deep sleep we may go back to an earlier stage in our evolution when we swung from branch to branch among the tree-tops.

And here, I think, the so-called flying dream has interest—the dream when you seem to be free of the body, floating through space, falling, dropping. Though this dream does not come to everybody, I know, it is of fairly general occurrence. No sensation of fear is present as you fall through empty space, but rather a feeling of enjoyment. There seems no purpose in your flight but merely the airy pleasure of careering through space without the encumbrance of a body. The nightmare touch is usually absent. Some people believe that unless they wake before the end with a crash-landing, it would mean death. Luckily, they always wake in time. Personally, I greatly enjoy my occasional flying dream, and wish I knew how to induce them, for I feel no fear of a final bump. In my case it is a recurrent dream with little or no variation.[3]

Talking of recurrent dreams there is one that haunts a friend of mine. He is a prominent public man whose name I will not mention. His dream has a particularly terrifying form. He is being led out to execution but before they reach the dreaded place his guards lead him to an even worse place where he is to be tortured. Had the German invasion materialised in 1940, as we all expected, my friend's name figured in a list of prominent men who were to be liquidated, but tortured first.

Well, we began talking about the fear of heights and have wandered off into the region of nightmares and recurrent dreams. But both these dreadful experiences have one thing in common—utter helplessness. You can't do anything about it. The muscles refuse to obey. This real helplessness seems to me the ultimate horror.

When I go to bed tonight, I hope no recurrent nightmare will return to hold me helpless, but that instead I shall enjoy a delightful flying dream.[4]

29 October 1947.

Notes

[1] Blackwood was a competent climber and would often undertake arduous climbs. Such feats and their consequences appear in several of his stories such as "Perspective" in *The*

Lost Valley (1910), where a fall leads to a mystical experience; or "Lost" in *Tongues of Fire* (1924), where the overwhelming presence of the mountains proves too much for one climber and he falls. Blackwood's passion for climbing is most tangible in "The Sacrifice" in *Incredible Adventures* (1914) where the pursuit of ascent becomes a metaphor of spiritual freedom.

[2] Samuel John Dixon (1852-1891) crossed the Falls twice, on 6 September 1890 and 17 July 1891. Blackwood could have seen him either time, but more likely the second. However, the small hotel Blackwood co-ran, The Hub, did not open until October 1891 so Blackwood could not have invited him there as the proprietor. In fact Dixon had attempted to swim across Wood Lake in the Muskoka region of Ontario on 2 October 1891 but got cramp and drowned.

[3] The flying dream is central to the plot of *Jimbo* (1909), where the eponymous young boy is trapped in a coma, menaced by various terrors in an empty old house, and his only way of escape is to learn to fly.

[4] I believe the individual he is referring to on the Nazi execution list was British diplomat and civil servant Robert, Lord Vansittart (1881-1947).

Superstition and the Magic "Curse"

The subject of magic has an inexhaustible attraction for the imaginative mind, though what precisely magic is, or claims to be, those so attracted would find it difficult to define. Its manifestations, at any rate, must occur according to clear-cut laws not only unknown to most of us, but unknown even to science.

These laws the magician, thanks to unusual study of himself in relation to nature, has presumably discovered. If science remains ignorant of them, this is due, claim the believers, to several facts. First, that science declines to study them, on the plea that no evidence worth study yet exists; second, that in the few instances where it has tried to study them, its method has been wrong; third, that only to a state of consciousness higher and more extended than our normal one can such knowledge be possible at all, and that the whole inquiry, therefore, lies outside the scope of science.

The popular interest in so-called Egyptian magic, stimulated by the recent tragedy to an excavator, has again proved that there are numerous intelligent persons who think that such higher states of consciousness, with their corollary of higher knowledge and strange powers, have been possible in the past, and are still accessible today.[1]

The ancients, they claim, favoured a line of inquiry foreign to our present-day mental attitude. The gulf, however, between such persons and those who are merely superstitious remains, I think, unbridgeable.

In the particular instance the method by which Egyptian magicians are thought to have protected their dead from violation seem to be secret poison or a curse. If poison, one would ask how this poison could be confined in its attack to a single individual only. If a curse, the whole question of thought, now so much in the public mind, comes under survey.

A curse is a violent and concentrated stream of thought of which ordinary minds are, fortunately, hardly capable. An ordinary "good-bye" ("God be with you") may have little virtue in it, whereas a similar blessing or curse, long sustained with passion, will, and the force of a powerful personality behind it, may certainly affect an impressionable mind against which it is directed. The power of thought, the effectiveness of suggestion, are to-day established for any open-minded person.

Both easily escape the label of superstition. But to credit an Egyptian magician of several thousand years ago with sufficient thought power to kill a man to-day is to lay a heavier burden upon a "curse" than it can bear.

9 April 1923.

Note

[1] This article was prompted by the death of the Earl of Carnarvon on 5 April 1923, just four days before. Blackwood, though, refers to an "excavator", and there was a rumour at the time that on the night Carnarvon died there was a blackout in Cairo and the next day bodies of two labourers who had worked on the excavation were found.

The Psychology of Places

The considerable role played by the psychology of places in certain temperaments must produce a noticeable extension of their gamut of feeling—the "note" of pleasure or pain, I mean, they receive from even the common places of the world. For, where many can pass through a given stretch of landscape untouched, these others may receive from the same space a series of impressions varying through every shade of emotion from exaltation to depression. Every "note" produces a reaction. The barrenest mile brings meaning. A tree that to one temperament "brings tears of joy", to another is but "a green thing standing in the way".

Yet, the hidden causes that prompt this perception of the psychology of places rest upon something far more profound and subtle than the mere love of Nature—upon a million delicate decisions, probably, of ancestral and utterly primitive origin. "I do not like thee, Dr. Fell; The reason why I cannot tell," appeals to everyone, of course; but, whereas most of us are quick to get the "note" of a *person*, for like or dislike, it has been my experience that only a few respond vividly to the "note" of a place— appreciate the psychology of places, that is.

With towns and the inhabited spots of the world it is easily traceable to definite causes. Going from one town to another is similar to going from one person to another for conversation in a room. Each in turn draws out a different aspect of the personality and, whether you like it or not, an unconscious readjustment of your inner world and forces takes place automatically. You present instinctively another front, though without any loss necessarily of sincerity in the process. You show new wares to a new customer, pushing others, felt "not wanted", below the counter. Leaving London one kind of man, you find two days later in Paris that you are another kind of man—showing at least a different grouping of emotions to the sun. And, later still, in Vienna and Pesth, a further readjustment has taken place, and the emotional kaleidoscope has shaken into view an aspect of your personality very different from the one that left the murk of heavy London behind a week before. With the towns this is all very obvious and analysable, although it has always seemed to me as significant—the beginning of a simple variant of the amazing phenomenon of multiple personality, and the difficulty sensitive natures find in knowing which is really their true self.

But with regard to the uninhabited regions of the world, the interest in this question of the psychology of places deepens and complicates at once. I have watched its operation in a thousand cases, yet never found any satisfactory explanation, outside the region of mystical theories, upon which one may not draw to beg the question. In the trackless Canadian forests the backwoodsman, experienced in all the essentials of woodcraft, who acts as your guide, invariably takes the "note" of a new camp before he allows you to settle down, and while a dozen practical details (wood, wind, water, fall of land, &c.) may seem to determine his decision alone, I have always noticed that a dozen unknown and unguessed causes contribute their element as well—things he can only shrug his shoulders over without reply. Almost as though some places grow a crop of big invisible query marks like trees, each demanding a satisfactory answer before one can settle for the night in comfort—and safety. And to watch these primitive men choose their resting-place has always suggested to me the actions of a wild animal wandering to and fro before it selects a lair; or the behaviour of a domestic beast, such as a cat or dog, before it curls up in a corner of the room and finally deposits itself in *the* right place.

One man in particular I remember (my companion in more than one of the desolate places of the world) who had this curious instinct unusually developed. He went through a regular ceremonial—unconsciously—before settling down and proclaiming the camp all right. Every essential of a good camp might be present, yet he was not satisfied until he had nosed about, explored and investigated a dozen vague conditions he seemed to "sense" yet could never have named; it almost suggested the survival of some deep atavistic tendency to placate the deities of the place before it was safe to eat and sleep there. Certain innate objections and predilections he had that clamoured to be satisfied before he felt really at home; and one of these—about the only one I ever heard him describe definitely—was "Never pitch your camp on the edge of anything; put the tent in the wood or out of it, but never on the borderland between the two."

And his objection, though laughingly expressed, was deep-seated and genuine; he was invariably consistent; and, while a man of normal modern culture, free from any shadow of superstition, he clung to this particular shibboleth with a tenacity that has often set me thinking since. Instinctively, and by no process logically worked out to a conclusion, I think he said a true thing there. For a threshold is ever the critical frontier that invites adventure and therefore possible disaster. The frontier, the entrance, the gateway, of course, sets the line between two opposing things, and may mean passing towards an attack from the unknown conditions that lie beyond. "On the edge of a wood," he said to me once as we lay round a camp-fire in the wilds, while I pressed him for an explanation of his feeling, "the tent stands on the very line where two sets of forces meet—the forces of the wood and the forces of the open. It is not a place of rest, but of activity. I like being right in the wood, or right out in the open."[1]

His words, suggesting the strip of unclaimed ground between the fringes of hostile armies, made us smile, while at the same time every man in the party recognised that he was right, and that what he said about the ethics of pitching a tent was, indeed, true of all frontiers and gateways. The psychical aspect of a threshold is essentially thrilling: the critical character of the very act of entrance announces itself instantly in any nature not utterly dead to the finer sensibilities. The moment the doorposts are left behind— of a railway carriage, your dentist's house, an afternoon call even!—the adventure has begun. It is the moment of birth, of life, thrill, excitement. The pre*limen*aries are over; you have entered the Unknown. And though a boundary line is, of course, a merely theoretic conception without actual existence, its invention is due to that fundamental need of human nature that seeks some kind of measurement by which to check its retrogression or advance. The feeling which prompted the Roman husband to carry his wife across the *limen* of his house, after which she should tread no more her own *fines* as a separate individual, is a manifestation of the same instinct that forbade my camping friend to pitch his tent upon an imaginary frontier-line; the same again, doubtless, which in the deeper regions of the soul-life has erected another more terrible gateway between two worlds and crystallised the emotion born of it into that haunting and awesome embodiment of warning—the Dweller on the Threshold.

30 April 1910.

Note

[1] The connection between the thoughts expressed in this article and Blackwood's story "The Willows" (1907) need hardly be emphasised.

Dreams and Fairies

The robot civilisation towards which we are now heading at ever increasing speed offers hardly standing room for either dreams or fairies as a source of literary inspiration. The racial consciousness, which the artist makes articulate, can express only what it contains; and if dream and fairy still exist, they are certainly somewhat moribund, the latter possibly quite dead, killed finally by the ridicule of photography. That once magical potency, at any rate, has evaporated so far as the imaginative writer is concerned. The racial consciousness, flashing headlong at so many miles per hour, finds no time to dream. Even the child now questions its fairy faith.[1]

The change has been rapid; there has been no long-drawn lingering illness; and probably it was Swan-Edison who struck the first shrewd blow when their electric light became universal and destroyed the long, dark evenings. Dusk, shadows, eerie half-lights vanished from the world which now shows too many sharp edges, lines devoid of suggestion, and clear-cut shapes as empty of mystery as Swiss scenery and with as merciless an atmosphere. For Switzerland, though it has produced Carl Jung, a great interpreter of dreams, has produced as few imaginative artists as fairies. Superstition anyhow, once picturesque and often pregnant, has lost calibre; it is grown stupid, even gross; while mystery, apart from the banal form of "thrillers", is becomes a reproach of ignorance, rather than the womb whence some fantastic progeny of fairyland might emerge.

This glaring light of the twentieth century, dissipating obscurity, annihilating the shadows of the mind, making of mystery a negative instead of a very positive element, may be actually, however, only changing our dreams and fairies into new forms of far more remunerative, if perhaps less lovely, kinds. The poet turns nowadays to machinery, speed, electricity and electrons, because the racial consciousness is concerned with these. The magi of today are physicists, the fairies rays, the magic carpet is space-time, while waves of ether have replaced the abracadabra of the old delightful wizard. What is lost in beauty, it seems, is to be gained in usefulness, and whether the new inspiration shall enrich or impoverish us eventually, whether mystery is to be deepened into a nobler type of wonder, or merely taken wholly away, only the future race will know.

Yet each kind engenders its own specific reaction, and fairy loveliness has nothing to say to usefulness. Some must remember the glamour and beauty that stole back into our darkened streets when the War put out the lights. That glamour lingers now chiefly in the great dim forests of the world, whence the fairies originally issued in remote time, and into which they have now certainly withdrawn again. Once these dim vasty forests have, in their turn, been cut down to make way for cities or garden plots, they will perhaps retire, with their gauze and haunting music, into the bowels of the earth which will take longer to excavate, or into the unplumbed deeps of the sea where no hostile light can penetrate. Having once deserted the consciousness of men, however, it is of small interest where they go or what becomes of them. Humans, no longer aware of them, will not even ask a question.

Everything possible to be believed, said Blake, is an image of truth, but if a certain type of image no longer presents itself, the poet and the artist will not sing to us about them. If Shakespeare were alive today, at one with the central energies of life as he was, could he have written *A Midsummer Night's Dream*? He made articulate the essential deeps of the racial consciousness of his day. "He was born," John Masefield reminds us in his Romanes Lecture on "Shakespeare and the Spiritual Life", "into a superstitious country society at a time when the land was undrained, the roads unpaved, and the winter nights unlighted.[2] From November till March travelling after dark was almost impossible. People sat by the fire and told stories of fairies, witches and ghosts who then made life terrible all over the countryside. Besides these things, there were other things. If, like St. Withold, you 'footed thrice the wold', you were likely to meet the Night Mare and her ninefold.[3] The wold was only three or four miles from Stratford, up Meon Hill: the Night Mare ran there with her ninefold. In that underpopulated England the Night Mare and her ninefold had a wide range of pasture." And he adds, significantly: "It was a long way between churches." Here was the atmosphere that engendered fairies and their delightful brood, an atmosphere that Swan, Edison and Co. have certainly helped to dissipate.

The collective consciousness of the race is now otherwise. Only among the side-eddies of creation do we find the Little People unless, as with Yeats, A.E., and some others, a definite corner of the earth, a particular land or people, with their own specific dreams and fantasies, are being sung. *A Fairy Leapt Upon my Knee*,[4] charmingly rendered, is after all only *about* a fairy that is not a fairy at all in the true sense, and is even less fairy-ish than *Still She Wished for Company* where Miss Irwin made something of

Einstein's space-time articulate with astonishing success and still more astonishing atmosphere.[5] *Lolly Willowes*, of course, is neither ancient nor modern but just successfully itself.[6] Arthur Machen, on the other hand, uses Magic with all the older power; and *Vathek*, farther back of course, has the unearthly touch at full strength, its amazing speed confirming its strange inspiration. For much the same reason the "Brushwood Boy" entrances.[7]

About a certain type of vivid dream there hangs an atmosphere of the unearthly that hints, as J. W. Dunne suggests in his *Experiment with Time*, at a different state of consciousness. Hence, perhaps, its haunting wonder. If fairy-stock has depreciated owing to the scientific spirit of modern life, dream-stock has in certain ways gone up in value. If psychoanalysis, without adding much to our really useful knowledge, has robbed dreams of their gossamer and glamour, it has in another way increased our interest in them. The modern study of that terrifying cavern, the subconscious, has revealed something of the strange mechanism at work below the surface. An emotion, or vivid impact, received on the surface is not forgotten, but apparently sinks down to be stored forever. The subconscious tends to dramatise all such. If God geometrises, the subconscious dramatises, the former slogan ancient, the latter modern. Coleridge asleep, whether it was natural or induced sleep, dramatises what he had recently received, and produced "Kubla Khan"; William Archer catches his "Green Goddess" from a remembered dream;[8] R.L.S. and a host of others report similar experiences.[9] The artist, as we call him, seems to be the type of mind that can recover this subconscious content, express it in paint or words or music, make it articulate.

I remember a writer in Egypt whose imagination had been vividly and painfully impressed by a case of someone dying of thirst in the desert.[10] This lack of water was in his mind when he fell asleep. He woke in the morning with a singular phrase running in his head: "You will drown, but will not know you drown." Guessing this was the climax of a story that lay *complete* in him, he began a tale, hoping for the best. Only when he neared the end did the odd phrase justify itself. His emotion of the previous night had dramatised itself in sleep, but had poked up, so to speak, with its end first. The Familiar, the Dæmon, it seems, have changed their names into the Subconscious and the Subliminal Self. It is a case of too much explaining possibly: explaining becomes so easily explaining away. Beginning with *The Time Machine* down to *Thunder on the Left*, the inspiration behind dream- and fairy-stories is scientific, metaphysical, philosophical.[11] Books like A.E.'s *Candle of Vision* are rare, too rare. There seems no antidote.

Yet there is one thing scientific dreams and fairies cannot do—they cannot "terrify". There lies no purging by lovely terror in their calculated spell, for their inspiration is mechanical, not divine. The "Lordly Ones" of the "Immortal Hour", the Sidhe, are "terrible" because they are other-worldly and not of this earth. Ariel as a personified wave-length we listen to in our drawing-rooms, the "sightless couriers of the air" as waves of ether bringing us sound or pictures through a machine costing so many pounds—these, though wonderful, hold no wonder of the *spirit*. The wonder of the spirit is not the wonder of the well-read mind. The purchaser questions, but he does not tremble with delicious and unearthly awe.

Today our winds seem thin of voices, our woods and forests emptying, our glens feed streams where dance no flashing feet. The haunting music of that older world is stilled and no wings dart across the moonlight that once was populated with haunting glory. It may be, however, that the glamour is but changing and that the poet's creative heart will extract a more stimulating Wonder from the newer "facts" of life. Mystery, of course, there must always be. The change is worth underlining—it will be a Wonder that *instructs*; a Wonder that teaches before it beautifies. In which connection another word from Masefield's Romanes Lecture is most significant: "A seer once said to me," he mentions, " 'If a man tells you he has seen the fairies, look if he be shaken. If he be not terrified, be sure that he has not seen.' "

December 1929.

Notes

[1] Blackwood re-emphasises here, in this 1929 essay, the same sentiments that he expressed in *The Centaur* (1911), where he said, in part, after the main character had read a newspaper report listing both scientific progress and disasters: " . . . it was not the contrast which made him smile; rather was it the chance juxtaposition of certain of the contents; for on the page facing the accounts of railway accidents, of people burned alive, explosions, giant strikes, crumpled air-men and other countless horrors which modern inventions offered upon the altar of feverish Progress, he read a complacently boastful leader that extolled the conquest of Nature men had learned *by speed*. The ability to pass from one point to another across the skin of the globe in the least possible time was sign of the development of the human soul."

[2] The Romanes Lecture, named after George John Romanes, who delivered the first in 1891, is an annual lecture given at the University of Oxford by invitation to a distinguished

authority in the fields of art, science or literature. John Masefield's lecture in 1924 was "Shakespeare and Spiritual Life" which became available as a separate booklet.

[3] Blackwood is quoting Masefield who is himself quoting from Shakespeare's *King Lear*.

[4] *A Fairy Leapt Upon My Knee*, published in 1927, was very popular at the time, which may be why Blackwood did not name the author, Bea Howe (1898-1992). She was a close friend of Sylvia Townsend Warner—see note 6. The novel is about how a fairy influences the relationship between a young couple.

[5] *Still She Wished for Company* (1924) was the first novel by Margaret Irwin (1889-1967) and brings together the lives of two women who live almost 250 years apart, but whose experiences start to overlap.

[6] *Lolly Willowes* (1926) was the first novel by Sylvia Townsend Warner (1893-1978) and is dedicated to her friend Bea Howe—see note 4. It concerns a woman who seeks her own freedom and lifestyle even though this may mean becoming a servant of Satan.

[7] *Vathek* (1786) is the noted, perhaps even notorious, Gothic-Oriental novel by William Beckford (1760-1844) about a caliph's attempts to master the powers of the supernatural. "The Brushwood Boy" (1895) is a novella by Rudyard Kipling about a boy maturing in a world of dreams. It is testament to Blackwood's faith in his readers that he feels he does not always need to identify the author because the works he cites are so well known.

[8] *The Green Goddess* was a stage play and later movie written by theatre critic William Archer (1856-1924), first performed in 1920. It prefigured *Lost Horizon* by having a group of English people crash into a remote Himalayan society.

[9] R.L.S. is, of course, Robert Louis Stevenson according to whom *Strange Case of Dr. Jekyll and Mr. Hyde* (1886) was inspired by a dream which he wrote about in "A Chapter on Dreams" (1888).

[10] The writer is Blackwood himself and the story was "By Water", collected in *Day and Night Stories* (1914). He writes more about the origins of this story in "The Birth of an Idea", reprinted in this volume.

[11] *The Time Machine* (1895) is, of course, by H. G. Wells. *Thunder on the Left* (1925) by Christopher Morley which compares, in fantasy terms, the differences between growing old and eternal youth.

Explorers' Ghost Stories

Genuinely true ghost stories are hard to come by, as anyone who takes the trouble to track them to their origin may know. They have a way of becoming less convincing, less impressive, the nearer one draws to their source. Often enough they evaporate completely. A true ghost story, honestly told, always thrills; and some of the best I have found in books of travel and exploration where the traveller, bent upon quite other matters and probably not even interested in other-worldly things, has come across a queer happening and set it down honestly and faithfully. Having read several such experiences in books of this kind, I have jotted them down. They may interest others as they did me.

The narrators, as a rule, are hard-headed men, who have warmed both hands at the fires of life. Most of them have looked bright-eyed danger in the face without blinking. They have been "up against it" in a thousand ways. They hold life cheap. Their books, respectively, prove them men of courage and resource. And when men of this stamp tell a queer story and vouch for its veracity, the story is usually impressive. Not all of the tales I shall quote from are, strictly speaking, ghost stories, but all are interesting, suggestive and, to say the least, mighty queer. They happened both on sea and land. To take a sea experience first . . .

It is described in *A Gypsy of the Horn*, where Rex Clements tells of his voyage in a windjammer round the world some twenty years ago.[1] The queer incident may be found on page 129 *et seq.*, and it occurred in the Pacific soon after leaving Chatham Island. The weather for days had been severe, even terrible, but the ship at last had run into calmer water.

"One dark, moonless night," says the author, "just before we got clear of the 'Forties, with a fresh breeze blowing, and the ship running quietly along under t'gallants'ls, there occurred a most uncanny experience.

"It was about four bells in the middle watch, the 'churchyard watch' as the four hours after midnight is called, that it happened. We, of the mate's watch, were on deck, the men for'ard, Burton and I under the break, and Mr. Thomas pacing the poop above our heads. Suddenly, apparently close aboard on the port hand, there came howling out of the darkness a most frightful, wailing cry, ghastly in its agony and intensity. Not of over-powering volume—a score of men shouting together could have raised as loud a hail—it was the indescribable calibre and agony of the shriek that almost froze the blood in our veins."

All rushed to the rail, mate and men too, and stared into the blackness to windward. "The starbowlines, tired men asleep in their bunks below, poured up on deck. If ever men were horror-struck, we were. Even the Old Man was awakened by it, and came up on deck to see. All listened, eyes strained. A moment or two passed— then the appalling scream rang out again, rising to the point of almost unbearable torture and dying crazily away in broken whimperings. No one said a word. All stood like stones, peering into the gloom. The sound was not repeated. Slowly, at length, like men emerging from a trance, we moved and spoke. The men sat up all night, unable to sleep . . . "

Many guesses, the author goes on to say, were hazarded as to the explanation of the awful, terrifying cry, but none of them seemed satisfactory to anybody. The cry of a whale was suggested, "but I never heard a whale utter any sounds with its throat," is the writer's comment. Some sea monster that only rarely comes to the surface? "More unlikely still." The scream of seals, or of sea-lions, on an island beach? Yet the nearest land was Easter Island, six hundred miles to the north! The shriek, moreover, as all who heard it agreed, was "so human". Was it a shipwrecked boat's crew?

The uncanny sound was never explained. Its effect upon all concerned, from the captain downwards, lasted for days. "In bare words," adds the author, finally, "it doesn't sound very terrible, but it made that night a night of terror, and even now it sends a shiver through me to think of it."

A sound that keeps the crew of a windjammer out of their beds all night and puts the fear of God into the ship's officer as well, to say nothing of the Old Man, may well have been of a fairly convincing nature! The incident, taken out of its full context, and apart from the atmosphere of an enthralling book, loses, of course, something of its impressiveness. It has, however, the true ring about it. That cry was heard by a large number of hard-headed men; it scared them badly; and explanation there was none.

While on the subject of queer noises, whether auditory hallucinations or otherwise, two other cases are worth mentioning, both of them in high mountains.

The first is told by the famous rock-climber George D. Abraham, the author of many thrilling books of mountain adventure, and the hero of more than one escape. He was in a hut on the Dôm, 9,400 feet up, with a couple of porters. "Just at twilight," he writes, "a curious thing happened. We were all sitting round the cold stove, wrapped in blankets, when a terrible human yell, as of pain, sounded outside, quite close to the hut, and just for a moment it caused the bravest of us to shudder. Two of us wrenched open the snowed-up door, fully expecting to revive someone in distress. However, nothing was visible but dense snow clouds and no human traces could be seen near the hut. The two porters were in a state of collapse and did little but mutter '*Geister*! *Geister*!' with other expressions in patois signifying that the whole party was doomed. Nothing would suffice but that they must descend to the valley at once and leave me (with my guide) to finish the climb, which they felt now would be our last." The porters were seen down into safety, while the author and his guide spent a cold and sleepless night in the hut, but did not hear the yell again, nor ascertain what caused it. No disaster followed, at any rate, beyond the minor one that the porters' heavy loads had to be borne by others.[2]

The story has its interest. Mountain guides and porters are not, as a rule, superstitious in the ghostly sense, although certain mountains, certain peaks rather, may enjoy an atmosphere that is malignant in their minds. The Matterhorn, until conquered, most certainly was haunted for the local peasants, this being due partly to its believed inaccessibility and terrifying rock falls, and partly, no doubt, to its dangerous and menacing aspect. It is no longer haunted now, Whymper having, if at an awful price, laid its evil spirit. In the case just described, it is significant that more than one man heard the strange cry, the same remark applying also to the shriek heard by the windjammer's crew. What one man hears may easily be set down as hallucination, but a collective hallucination is more difficult to accept. Mountains, on the other hand, are notorious for strange noises: wind, ice splitting off, rocks falling, snow settling (the dull boom of a snow-field settling is an unpleasant sound), to say nothing of the tricks that echo may play. Experienced climbers, on the other hand, are familiar with these odd sounds and could hardly ascribe them to a human yell.

Captain Gault MacGowan, F.R.G.S. and his wife, climbing in the Western Himalayas, have a similar tale to tell, though in this case it was a mysterious rifle shot that undoubtedly saved their lives.[3] The account must be condensed, although such condensation robs it of much interesting and exciting detail. MacGowan and his wife, for certain reasons, left their main party and undertook a very hare-brained (his own word!) climb on their own account. As the day was closing in they found themselves amid a waste of these immense and desolate mountains, in freezing cold, without provisions or shelter, lost at a great height. For hours they had adventures recklessly among gaping crevasses, along knife-edge crests, and across steep couloirs ending in a sheer drop into empty space. Both were exhausted, cold, hungry, when, having descended at grave risk a dangerous gradient, they reached a mighty crevasse impossible to cross. Turning to reclimb the awful slope, the smooth rocks they had slithered down proved unnegotiable. Unable to get up or down, they found themselves stuck. "Nearby was a hollow in the rocks. We crept into it and gazed at each other helplessly. It looked as if this was the end." Their predicament seemed hopeless, and a night at such an elevation, without food or dry clothing, must have ended in death.

"Suddenly across the snow spaces came the sharp crack of a rifle-shot! Imagine our relief! We realised at once that the *shikari* was somewhere near us and blessed him for his wisdom in firing the gun—our only means of communication. My wife turned the glasses in the direction of the shot and in two moments we had picked up the main party—four tiny black dots away across the glacier, high up on the opposite side of the valley. She took off her coat and waved it frantically and we shouted our loudest in chorus. Had they seen us . . . ?"

Several hours later, after some perilous scrambling in the deepening twilight, the two parties met and danger was over. "We congratulated the *shikari* on his forethought in firing the gun, for it had undoubtedly been the means of saving our lives. To our amazement, however, the man indignantly denied having fired his rifle. He seemed hurt that we should accuse him of doing so without permission and declared that he had heard no shot, the porters verifying his statement. Thereupon I counted the ammunition. It was untouched; the rifle was clean! There was no alternative but to believe that Providence had taken a hand on our behalf and the porters assured us emphatically that God had saved our lives."

The story invites none but rather obvious comment, perhaps. Of the three incidents described, that of the windjammer is the most convincing. A characteristic belonging to them all is noticeable, and perhaps significant: that the strange sounds were heard by men in a state of physical exhaustion. The ship's crew, after weeks of battling with terrific weather, were worn out, and climbers at the end of a long day which had started probably before dawn, are in a condition of severe bodily fatigue. Nerves and muscles are both weary.

The other cases of queer or ghostly happenings that I have jotted down from my reading are, I think, of a more interesting and significant kind—more convincing, at any rate. Two of them combine visual with audible experiences; the tangible being, however, not included: though being, perhaps, the rarest of qualities met with in a ghost story, or the sense most difficult to affect. When all three senses are impressed, to say nothing of smell and taste, the result may be considered highly interesting, though not necessarily more evidential.

Commander H. G. Stoker, D.S.O., R.N., gives a curious account of a visible appearance in his book *Straws in the Wind*, when he describes his escape with two companions from the Turkish Prison Camp at Hissar, in the centre of Asia Minor and 130 miles from the nearest sea. The characteristic of physical exhaustion and intense nervous strain is again noticeable, as will be seen. Captain Stoker, of course, was in charge of the famous submarine *AE2* during the war, whose exploits were well known—a man of great daring and resource.[4] Two officer friends of his on the submarine had lost their lives some eighteen months before the uncanny experience to be described: during the escape, as he frankly tells us, he mistook his two companions in flight for these two dead men, addressing them as such even in daylight, "while realising the absurdity of the obsession and recognising it was an hallucination". The over-wrought condition of mind and nerves is frankly admitted, yet the visible appearance, the ghost, which was seen by him when in this state, was seen by his two escaping pals as well. Here is the point of interest in this curious account. We hear much about "extended telepathy" nowadays. Did Commander Stoker's strong personality transfer a visual hallucination of his own to the receptive minds of his two companions? He goes into little detail concerning it, merely giving a straightforward description of what occurred. He mentions, however, that the whole time the ghostly figure was visible—several hours—he kept the fact to himself. It was later that he discovered from a spontaneous remark of his companions that they both had seen the figure too. The appearance, he declares, differed wholly from the obsession of his dead officer friends of the submarine. This latter he recognised as a pure hallucination.

To come, then, to his "queer" tale:

With two companions they escaped from the prison camp and got a fair start before their absence could be noticed and, in due course, after breathless experiences and hairbreadth risks, they reached the Taurus Mountains on their way to the sea. Only one pass was feasible, it was strictly guarded, sentries armed to the teeth prowled over its narrow neck, watch fires gleamed. One of their party would reconnoitre, and then the three of them would crawl past just out of reach of the dangerous fires. It was very dark, a wild night, a gale of wind whistling through the crags. The sense of danger, prolonged over several hours, was intense; another step and they might be challenged, shot at sight; but the storm muffled the noise of their stumbling among the rough stones and the sentries did not stray further than need be from their fires. Hunger, thirst, physical exhaustion, nervous and mental strain, all were severe. They moved in single file.

"In the middle of the night I felt—not suddenly nor surprisedly—that we were not three men struggling along in line, but *four*. There was a fourth man at the end of our line, in the correct position for a fourth man to be. When we stopped for a few moments' rest, he did not join us, but remained in the darkness, out of sight; yet as soon as we rose and resumed our march, he dropped into place forthwith. He never spoke, nor did he go ahead to lead us. His attitude seemed just that of the true and loyal friend who says 'I cannot help but, when danger is at hand remember always that I am here, to stand—or fall—with you.' "

The face is not seen, it will be noticed; no sound of footsteps stumbling among the rocks is audible; there is no detailed description of the figure, beyond that it is that of a man; nor is any attempt at speech recorded, either between the author and the ghostly appearance, nor between the author, again, and his two companions.

This mysterious fourth man stayed by them, following in line, until the worst was over and the dangerous pass had been successfully negotiated. The escaped prisoners reached the plain and breathed more freely. "I turned and looked behind," writes the author. "The fourth man had disappeared. I made no mention of him to the other two. A couple of hours later, drinking hot cocoa in a safe hiding place, one of my companions made a quiet remark about the fourth man. They had both seen him. We had all three been sensible of his presence throughout the most trying part of the night: we all three agreed that the moment he left us was when we felt we had put the danger behind . . . I cannot exaggerate," he adds, "how real his presence was, how content one felt—despite the mystery of it—that he should be there, what a strength and comfort his presence seemed to be. From the time he left us luck turned against us." Not long after, indeed, the whole party was recaptured and imprisoned again.

Having sent an account of the incident to Sir Arthur Conan Doyle, Commander Stoker received the following reply: "It is the same experience as Shackleton's sledge party, which had an extra man. One of you was probably mediumistic (without knowing it). Many are. Some friend took advantage of the fact."

In *The Lure of the Labrador Wild*, one of the most poignantly moving adventure books ever written, a very interesting case of other-worldly intervention in human affairs is given. The volume describes with intense vividness the Leonidas Hubbard Expedition (1905) across Labrador, ending in Hubbard, its leader, being starved to death in the most distressing circumstances.[5] Had the ghostly intervention been obeyed his life would unquestionably have been saved.

The expedition was on its way back, making as fast as their exhausted, half-starved condition would allow for

Grand Lake, where a cache of food lay waiting for them. Winter was setting in with its awful cold. They had been living on soup made out of old boots, decayed partridge, anything and everything that would yield the tiniest amount of sustenance in fact, for many days, and travelling over the roughest sort of country at the same time. Exhaustion had reduced them all to skeletons, and death was close. To work the canoe at all was almost beyond their strength and they had no idea what river they were on, nor where it led. Finally the question was faced: should they desert the river and cut across country in the last hope of making Grand Lake and the buried food?

There was a long discussion. The chances across country were against them for Hubbard could hardly walk by this time and the other two were feeble and emaciated; yet the river was against them too, for a long stretch of dangerous rapids lay ahead, and the men had no strength to deal with difficult water. An upset meant certain death. Besides, where was the river leading them? The discussion, a very keen but very friendly one, led to no decision, but Hubbard himself was in favour of the cross-country venture, desperate though it was. And Hubbard was leader of the expedition. In the end they decided to sleep on it.

The third member of this desperate party was George Elson, a half-breed Cree Indian from James Bay, engaged for the expedition by the Hudson Bay Company Post at Missanambie, Ontario. He was a stalwart in every sense of the term; a fine fellow, calm, cheerful, companionable, faithful, a man of character. He was, in addition, a man of immense experience. It was through this Indian that the "other-worldly intervention" came—a dream.

The morning following the discussion the three men renewed the fateful talk, in the course of which George announced: "I had a strange dream about it last night, fellas," he said quietly. He was asked to tell it.

"It was a strange dream," he repeated and hesitated. Hubbard urged him to go on. "Well, I dreamed the Lord stood before me, very beautiful and bright, and He had a mighty kind look on His face. And He said to me: 'George, don't leave this river. Just stick to it and it will take you out to Grand Lake, where you'll find the cache with lots of grub, and then you'll be all right and safe. I can't spare you any more fish, George, and if you leave this river you won't get any more. Just stick to this river and I'll take you out safe.' The Lord was all smilin' and bright, and He looked at me very pleasant. Then He went away and I dreamed we went right down the river and came out in Grand Lake, near where we had left it coming up. And we found the cache and all the grub we wanted, and had a fine time."

Dillon Wallace, the author of the book describing the expedition, adds: "It was quite evident that George was greatly impressed by his dream. I give it here simply for what it is worth. At the same time, I cannot help characterising it as remarkable, not to say extraordinary; for none of us had the faintest suspicion that the river we were on emptied into Grand Lake at all, much less that its mouth was near the point where we left the lake on our way up. But I myself attached no importance to the dream at the time, whatever I may think now."

Hubbard himself, an intensely religious man, also disregarded the dream which, if obeyed, would have saved his life. He admitted it was "unusual", but it did not turn him from his strong instinct to leave the river and cut across country. "It isn't possible, you know," he said to George, "for this river to empty into Grand Lake. We were talking about leaving the river last night, and you had it on your mind." Thus he explained the dream.

"Maybe," admitted the Indian, "but it was a mighty strange dream, and we'd better think about it before we leave the river. Stick to the canoe, Hubbard, that's what I say."

In the end Hubbard, too weak to move, sent Wallace and George across country, he himself remaining with what food there was in the little tent. The two men, after terrible privations, reached the cache of food but when, later, they arrived with help at the tent, they found Hubbard dead beside his diary. The few entries the dying Hubbard made in his diary during the last awful solitude are among the most moving and poignant imaginable. And, the river emptied into Grand Lake after all.

Two other capital true ghost stories carry us from bleak and frozen Labrador to the genial heat of the tropics— Borneo and New Guinea. Most of the European houses in Borneo, to take that first, are *berhantu* (haunted) according to the natives, and the following ghost story is told by Oscar Cook, late District Officer, North Borneo Civil Service, in his enchanting volume, *Borneo: Stealer of Hearts.*[6] The Commissioner, at a place called Tengilan, met his death suddenly by drowning, and Cook was summoned to replace him temporarily as Acting District Officer. It was 1917. Cook was invited to stay with another official in a comfortable little European house, which had been inhabited formerly by an Englishman named G. This man G., some years before, entangled by drink and a native woman, had died in the room—in the very bed indeed— Cook now occupied. Cook, himself, knew nothing of this, and his host did not mention it.

After a long talk about the immediate business in hand, the two men separated for bed at 10.30. Cook heard his host moving about in his room; they called good night to each other through the thin wooden walls; then Cook put his lamp out. He heard the clock strike eleven.

"Then I fell asleep," he writes. "Suddenly, I was wide awake, but not with a start. No sound of presence had aroused me. I was simply wide awake. I was not strung up, nor excited. I turned over and looked at my watch—it was after 1 a.m. (*I have somewhat condensed the following account of what happened. – A.B.*) I closed my eyes and was about to fall asleep again when I heard footsteps coming up the steps that led from the garden to the front door.

"I listened. Slowly the footsteps mounted the stairs. Then I heard the catch of the low wooden gate pulled back and the creak of the doors being opened. Down the full length of the veranda came the footsteps and passed into the dining-room. Whoever was walking kept straight on, for I heard the noise of the doors that shut off this room from the passage leading to the kitchen being opened, and the footsteps went along this passage. Then they halted.

"A clear and decisive voice then called out: 'Boy!' It was a voice I did not recognise. No answer came. Again the voice rang out, but in a sharper, more impatient tone: 'Boy!' Again there was no reply. After a brief silence, the footsteps then descended the stairs that led from the passage to the kitchen. They halted on the bottom step. 'Boy!' the voice called out angrily. There was no answer. Another silence followed. Then the footsteps came back up the stairs, passed along the passage again, across the dining-room and out onto the veranda. The creak of the gate reached me and I heard the closing of the latch. Down the steps the footsteps clumped and out into the garden. Then silence . . . I fell asleep, wondering who it was."

At breakfast next morning Cook asked his host what he was doing, walking all over the house during the night. "So you heard it too!" was the rejoinder, with relief. "I never moved all night long."

Cook stared at his host, an unimaginative man, a long-headed shrewd planter, a man of facts and figures and an utter scoffer at ghostly things. "Well," he asked, "what about it then?"

"It was G.," his host went on, "calling for a drink. I've often been disturbed by him. G. was the man here before my predecessor. He died in your room—on your bed. The doctor visited him one day, hearing he was ill. He gave him five minutes to live. Old G. just managed to sit up in bed, smiled, and asked for gin. He smoked a moment, chatted a bit, the gasper dropped from his lips—he was dead! He's buried in the garden, just on the slope of the hill below your window. My predecessor *saw* him, and one night even shot him. Well, there it is! My predecessor saw and shot him; I, too, have seen him; you've heard him. It's there, and it happens, and it's always the same. Now, get on with your tea, and we'll go and look at the grave. I always inspect it twice a month, and put a coolie to tend and clean it."

Captain A. W. Monckton, F.R.G.S., F.Z.S., tells a first-rate and most circumstantial ghost story in his widely read volume, *Some Experiences of a New Guinea Resident Magistrate*.[7] It is indexed as "Spooks in Samarai" and occurs on page 109. It is admirably told and as convincing as anything well can be. "I tell the story for what it's worth," he writes, sandwiching it in among other adventures of a most enthralling description. "I leave my readers who are interested in psychical research to form what opinion they choose. All I say is that the story, as related, is absolutely true." And, indeed, it has the ring of sincerity and truth all through it.

The author was staying alone in the house of a man named Moreton, at Samarai, Moreton living elsewhere at the time; he was Resident Magistrate of the Eastern Division.

"One night," runs the account, "in Moreton's house, I had a curious and uncanny experience. I was sitting at the table, writing a long dispatch which engaged all my attention; my table was in the middle of the room, and on my right and left hand respectively there were two doors, one opening on to the front and the other on to the back veranda of the house. Both doors were closed and fastened with ordinary wooden latches, which could not possibly open of their own accord as a spring lock might do. The floor of the room was made of heavy teakwood boards, nailed down; the floor of the veranda being constructed of laths of palm, laced together with native string.

"As I wrote, I became conscious that both doors were wide open and—hardly thinking what I was doing—I got up, closed them both, and went on writing. A few minutes later I heard footsteps upon the coral path leading up to the house; they came across the squeaky palm veranda, my door opened, and the footsteps went across the room and—as I raised my eyes from my dispatch—the other door opened, and the footsteps passed across the veranda and down again on to the coral. I paid very little attention to this at first, having my mind full of the subject of which I was writing, but half thought that either Poruma or Giorgi (trusted personal servants), both of whom were in the kitchen, had passed through the room. However, I again rose and absent-mindedly shut both doors for the second time.

"Some time later, once more the footsteps came, crash-crash on the coral, squeak-squeak on the veranda; again my door opened and the squeak changed to the tramp of booted feet on the boarded floor. As I looked to see who it was, the tramp passed close behind my chair and across the room to the door, which opened, and then again the tramp changed to a squeak and the squeak to the crash on the coral. I was, by this time, getting very puzzled but, after a little thought I decided my imagination was playing me tricks and that I had not really closed the doors when I thought I had. I made certain, however, that I did close them this time and went on with my work again. Once more, the whole thing was repeated, only this time I rose from the table, took my lamp in my hand and gazed hard at the places on the floor from which the sound came, but could see nothing."

Captain Monkton then describes how he went on to the veranda and bawled to the two servants in the kitchen, asking who was playing tricks and, before they could answer, steps again sounded in his room behind him. Poruma, hearing the steps, was surprised. "I didn't know you had anyone with you," he observed, whereupon his master repeated what had happened. "Someone keeps opening my door," he said, "and walking about. I want him caught."

Anyone who has read the book will know that Captain Monckton's orders generally *were* obeyed, without delay, too! But Poruma, the old servant, replied: "No one would dare to enter the government compound and play tricks on the Resident Magistrate." His master insisted angrily that the fellow, whoever he might be, must be caught. "I mean to get to the bottom of this fooling," he said, repeating his order. He sent to the guard house and got the gatekeeper, also the gaoler and all his warders, finally to the ship as well for men. The gatekeeper, an honest fellow, swore that the gate had been locked as usual at 10 p.m., before which hour none but government people had passed in.

A search under Captain Monckton's instructions was at once organised. There were only three rooms, furnished with Spartan simplicity. They were soon examined. Four men with lanterns were placed under the house, which was raised about four feet from the ground on piles. Other men were stationed back and front. Then the Captain searched the house once more himself. "It was impossible," he adds, "for a mouse to have passed unseen." This done, he shut the doors of his room, and sat inside with Poruma and Giorgi. They waited in silence a few minutes.

"Presently, exactly the same thing occurred once more. Through that line of men came the footsteps; through my room in precisely the same manner came the tread of a heavily booted man, then went on to the palm veranda where—in the now brilliant illumination—we could *see the depression at the spots from which the sound came*, as though a man were stepping there. (*The italics are my own. – A.B.*)

" 'Well,' I asked my men, 'what do you make of it?'

" 'No man living could have passed unseen,' was Poruma's reply. 'It's either the spirit of a dead man, or a devil.' "

Whatever Captain Monckton may have thought, and he offers no opinion or explanation, he moved to the ship for the night and slept on board. Nothing of the sort ever happened again, and a year later the house was pulled down. Before this, however, the author had sat up in it on purpose with a man named Armit, Health Officer and Collector of Customs, but the investigation produced no results. Armit, on this occasion, mentioned that Moreton, the former occupant, had once or twice hinted at something queer having happened. Moreton himself was therefore interviewed on the subject. His reply was interesting:

"One night," he admitted, "sleeping in a hammock on the veranda, I heard footsteps. They wakened me. I called out angrily, 'Who's making the racket?' There was no reply, but my hammock was banged violently against the wall. I said nothing about it to anyone, for I was alone at the time, and I didn't want to be laughed at."[8]

July 1925.

Notes

[1] Reginald ("Rex") Clements (1885-1961) served his apprenticeship aboard the *Arethusa*, one of the last of the windjammer sailing ships which plied its trade from England to Australia. His book *A Gypsy of the Horn* (1924) recounts his experiences twenty years earlier, so around 1903-4 or earlier, when he was in his mid-late teens.

[2] Blackwood does not cite the source, so he may have read this when it appeared as an article "Adventures in the High Alps" by George D. Abraham (1871-1965) in *The Badminton Magazine* (January 1905). It was later incorporated in *The Complete Mountaineer* (1907).

[3] Again Blackwood cites no source and it's likely he read this as the article "To the 'End of the World' and Beyond" by MacGowan in *The Wide World Magazine* (May 1925). MacGowan (1894-1970) became a noted war correspondent during World War II but in the First World War and early 1920s he served with the British Light Army in India.

[4] Commander Henry Hugh Gordon Dacre Stoker (1885-1966), the author of *Straws in the Wind* (1925) was a cousin of Bram Stoker. He was a noted sportsman but served in the Royal Navy from 1900 to 1920, and again at the outbreak of the Second World War. Stoker commanded the submarine *AE2* which was torpedoed by the Turks in 1915 and he spent the rest of the war in the prisoner of war camp discussed here.

[5] *The Lure of the Labrador Wild* (1905) was written by Dillon Wallace (1863-1939) a New York lawyer and adventurer

who was asked by Leonidas Hubbard (1872-1903) to join his expedition to explore Labrador. That expedition was in 1903, not 1905 as Blackwood dates it. The 1905 expedition—in fact there were two—were led separately by Wallace himself, and by Hubbard's widow Mina.

[6] Oscar Cook (1888-1952) was a government official in British North Borneo from 1911 to 1919 out of which came his book *Borneo: Stealer of Hearts* (1924). It was through this book that he met his future wife Christine Campbell Thomson (1897-1985), noted as the editor of the *Not at Night* series of anthologies. Through Thomson, Cook sold several short horror stories starting with "Golden Lilies" (1922) and several appeared in the legendary US pulp *Weird Tales*, of which the best known was "Si Urag of the Tail" (July 1926), purportedly based on real events in Borneo.

[7] Captain Charles Arthur Monckton (1872-1936) was born in and lived most of his life in New Zealand where his father, a physician, had emigrated from England in the late 1860s. Although he ran a farm in New Zealand he was better known as an administrator—and a rather ruthless one—and explorer. He was appointed as a Resident Magistrate in New Guinea in 1897 and later as High Sheriff and High Bailiff, and organised a highly efficient native armed constabulary. He served in India during the War and then settled in England. He wrote three books about his experiences in New Guinea of which the first, from which Blackwood quotes, was published in 1920 and went through many printings. His dominating and aggressive style of administration would suggest, as Blackwood implies, that the strange events he reports were not of his imagination.

[8] Blackwood would have been interested in the reference to Moreton. This was Matthew Henry Reynolds-Moreton (1847-1909) who was the uncle of Blackwood's old friend in Canada, Reginald Reynolds-Moreton (1869-1929).

The Lure of the Unknown

I.

What Nansen said of polar exploration in particular is true of all exploration: "It is a mighty manifestation of the power of the unknown over the mind of man." The lure remains insatiable, but the planet cannot remain inexhaustible. Already the signs of exhaustion are apparent. There are few fields left to conquer; most of the geographical riddles have been solved; largely speaking, only details remain to be determined.

An explorer seeking new ground must indeed think hard before he starts. Everest, though not actually won, holds no further secret; Lhasa is commonplace; the North and South Poles bear their flags and gravestones; A. J. Wavell has shown us the Holy Cities of Mecca and Medina (*A Modern Pilgrim in Mecca*, 1912). Colonel Rawling has tapped and mapped the sinister heart of New Guinea (*Land of the New Guinea Pygmies*, 1913), the secret of the Brahmaputra Gorges was read by Captains Bailey and Morshead just before the war. Puzzled how the great river breaks through the highest range on the globe, they expected to find "the most tremendous waterfall in the world", finding instead a hundred miles of marvellous gorges, but no huge fall. Mount McKinley in Alaska, Ruwenzori on the equator, wear veils no more upon their frozen faces for Mr. Belmore

Browne has overcome the former (*Conquest of Mount McKinley*, 1913), while Mr. Wollaston (*From Ruwenzori to the Congo*, 1908) has told us all about the latter from summit to foundation. The ghost of swindling Dr. Cook cheered them through desperate storms, clinging mists, and an earthquake near the top.

"Both," says John Buchan in his excellent book, summarising these epics of adventure (*Last Secrets*, 1923), "stand at the opposite poles of climate; both are outside the brotherhood of mountains . . . extravagances of Nature . . . an ice-peak near the Pole, and a range of Mountains of the Moon—veiled in steaming mists of the Line . . . The charm of the book *Ruwenzori* is its strangeness. It tells of a kind of mountaineering to which the world can show no parallel . . . glacier moraines tangled with monstrous growths and swelling the homely Alpine flora into portents."

The riddle of equatorial snows is solved. The main features of the Amazon Basin are likewise known, and the volumes describing them have already been noticed in these columns. "Asia holds one blank patch," Colonel Buchan tells us, "last of the great secrets, perhaps—the Desert of Southern Arabia between the Yemen and the Oman, in whose sandy and waterless recesses some great news may await the traveller . . . "

To those, however, who follow the records of travel and exploration there still remained one other mysterious, almost mythical, region in Africa. Rumour and romance both coloured it, a strange, remote, perhaps impenetrable region of gigantic craters, where even prehistoric monsters might have survived from Earth's earliest ages. That, too, has now fallen. Alexander Barns, F.R.G.S., has been there and has just published his two years' exploration in one of the most fascinating volumes ever printed. *Across the Great Craterland to the Congo* (1923), with its maps and a hundred photographs, is a sequel to his *Wonderland of the Congo* (1922) and describes the giant craters in Tanganyika Territory and the volcanoes of S.E. Congo, "with some account of the African apes, and the capture and training of elephants at Api". It is a modern fairy tale of wonder, romance, adventure and scientific facts.[1]

The largest of these gigantic craters, Ngorongoro, is formed by subsidence due to subterranean erosion. It is twelve miles in diameter, eighty-five miles round, 2,000 feet deep and holds 75,000 head of game which never leave it. The excitement of the party as, day by day, they approached its mighty rim, is understandable. They drew nearer and nearer, "surrounded by evidences of the creation of the world . . . passing through a broken country, gloomy and weird, with old blackened and matted primeval acacia forests on one side, and an extraordinary wealth of flowers and flowering shrubs on the other, till at last, beyond the final dark belt of forest", they found themselves "standing on a great eminence, the edge of the world, gazing down into a chasm so vast and presenting such novel features that our breath was taken away". They gazed across blue haze, now forest-clad and grassy, but once a mighty sea of boiling lava . . . Magdad Lake marking the position where the giant forces stopped. Then—the animals. "A *crush* of game, collected within this huge ring-fence . . . eighty-five miles round, yet the animals packed . . . our open-mouthed astonishment when we went down . . . the vastness, the novel surroundings, the brooding mystery, the teeming life . . . these animals in dense array . . . tails swishing and manes bristling . . . stood, pranced, galloped, snorted . . . thousands of blue wildebeest, zebra, gazelle, gnu . . . Across this colossal amphitheatre we walked for two hours through herds of game . . . the crater-plane was smothered with them, the flat surface of a sea of backs with an undercurrent of legs." There were ostrich, eland, oribi, lions, cheetahs, hyenas, jackals, baboons in troops of a hundred, and hippos by the pools of the lake. At camp that night a huge rhinoceros marched up to within 250 yards of the tents, lay down in sight of all and went to sleep. How they all found enough to eat, you ask? The floor of this monster crater was a "close mat of succulent red and white clover, standing knee high . . . "

The mystery of this stupendous crater pervades the book, though the lure of the unknown which drives men to desperate deeds (and women, too, for Mrs. Barns was of the party and her husband tells in a lighter moment how he bobbed her hair), coaxed the explorers roaming onwards through the Congo forests to the Mokoto Lakes and their still active volcanoes. They left this extensive volcanic plateau at a height of five thousand feet, honeycombed through its terraced length with craters of all sizes, from the largest in the world to fairy rings and blow-holes a few yards in diameter, and journeyed among polyglot peoples with strange customs and incredible habits. On every page something interesting or startling happens, and though space forbids a detailed route, an idea of the book's atmosphere may be gathered. There were flowers, for instance, on these tropical highlands: crater flowers—crinum lilies, pink and white geraniums, anemones four inches across, violet hibiscus nine feet high with flowers six inches across, orchids, arborescent heather. There were flies: the Kungu fly on Lake Kivu, in swarms and clouds a mile long and hundreds of feet high, and the greater Kungu fly, drifting to the light and shovelled up next morning in basketsful by the hundredweight . . . and elephant mosquitoes swarming over everything. There were giant forest-hogs and the "coughing roar of the great cats" eating the carcase of a dead rhino just outside the camp;

man-eating lions, so bold that they were known as daylight lions, large, tame, very fat from so much game. A dead zebra, used to attract these latter, attracted "hyenas like a flock of sheep". The man-eaters of the Marungu equal the "Man-Eaters of Tsavo" in thrill and terror, for they would "push into an empty native hut and wait for the owner's return", and a Mrs. de Ridder, wife of a Belgian oculist, who went out one morning to shoot buffalo, saw two lions, fired, killed one "and the noise put up nine more"— this brave woman, having been bitten and clawed, owed her life solely to her own amazing courage. These man-eaters, moreover, "were silent as the grave. We never heard them once, yet they were all about us." There were strange insects and reptiles: moths flying to the 800-candle-power lanterns . . . the Great Eyed Emperor looking like a large bat along the beams of light, with wings eight inches across . . . and huge Longicorn beetles nearly knocking the lamp over. Gorillas too: of herculean proportions, able to break a lion's neck with ease, over six feet high, with a sixty-inch chest, and arms that spanned eight feet . . . "clopping" on their chests with their fists, or uttering terrifying roars yet, oddly enough, always silent at night, "sleeping peacefully in the open, not quarrelling like the chimpanzees and baboons".

There were strange humans, too: the pastoral and wandering Masai, who inhabited the giant crater were quiet folk, but others were repulsive, degraded by superstition, thick with witch-doctors, fetishism of all sorts, living in ghost-forests, people of debased and inferior type "looking at us with lowered eyelids". At Kondoa was a native who smeared his skin with some sort of vegetable oil, rendering it impervious to fire—"only a pleasant warmth without a mark" resulting. There were members too of the terrible Human Leopards Society, who eat human flesh killed as a leopard kills, with teeth and claw, steel knives fashioned like claws being attached to the wrists.[2] There were monstrosities sometimes, which the author was expected to cure: a man with two thumbs, odd cases of elephantiasis, and a woman whose nose had been bitten off by her husband, then stuck on again by plastering it with liquid rubber. The writer cured his own sciatica by a method which "deserves world-wide publicity"—the internal use of iodine—"recommended by the White Fathers of the R. C. Mission at Lulenga". The natives of a certain village he could not help, however . . . living among swarms of daylight lions, with only sticks and bludgeons for defence . . . nothing so gruesome as human remains after a lion has fed on them . . . "a rag, a bone, and a hank of hair".

So the amazing journey goes on through this wonderland of mystery and adventure, details of valuable scientific observation ever keeping pace with imaginative description. The varied scene lives before the eye. One day the party are rubbing their boots with dubbin made from lion fat, while "the magnificent chorus of lions echoes from the cliffs" about them; the next day they are camped by a spur of rock "thickly overgrown with the most enormous candelabra euphorbia I have ever seen, of great age, forty feet high, trunks eighty inches in diameter". A few weeks later, after thrilling accounts of hunting the great apes, they are watching the capture and training of elephants at Api, yet able to report that there is "no immediate possibility of the African elephant being exterminated, as the numbers have increased prodigiously of late years".

Another adventure takes us to the Valley of the Bees and, after that, we chase a magical butterfly, the Antizox, the most gorgeous in the world, thrilled by a glimpse of one, but never catching it.[3] "Who shall say that romance is dead?" the author exclaims—then adds his oft-repeated plea for the protection of the wild animals, especially the great apes. For the explorer's health he also has a word: "If mosquito nets are used, and quinine taken regularly with an evening peg of whisky, a man's health need not suffer (in the tropical towns)—if his constitution is good to start with." And there is a passage, rather hidden away, which betrays the true explorer-enthusiast: "The neighbourhood of a really big tropical African river always gives me a feeling of satisfaction. Its wildness and savagery have an irresistible appeal. The mere smell of the place, with its surroundings of mimosa thorn, palms and feathery grass, is soothing. The flowing water, the wild fowl, hippos grunting, and the lions' moaning call, are sounds that strike a sympathetic chord not unconnected, perhaps, with man's amphibian ancestry. I sometimes wish I had never come under this spell, for its call is nothing short of distracting and will remain as long as life lasts. With me it is an obsession."

The value of this delightful book is further increased by an introduction describing the origin of the gigantic crater written by Professor J. W. Gregory of Glasgow University.

II.

The lure of the unknown exercises its attraction also in another field of experience and one where travel, so far, has proved unremunerative, since science, scornfully, lends no hand.

It is apparent to any thinking mind that we live in a Universe only partially known. Our knowledge is limited by the reports of the imperfect senses, or by instruments which extend these senses. In its entirety we know nothing; if we did, that knowledge would be incommunicable. Some think the Universe is four-dimensional, what we perceive being merely its aspect thrust down before our three-dimensional faculties. Whether this troublesome fourth dimension is space-time, *á la* Einstein, or whether it is a purely spatial new measurement, the fact remains that space and time are merely our restricted method of examining something which actually is independent of these. They remain forms of thought . . . We reach, at any rate, the notion that "the whole visible universe is electricity in a variable state of extreme agitation", and there we stop. We reach, similarly, the frontier death, and there too, we stop.

Of what comes after death, if anything, we have no data. Books multiply, but facts remain unascertainable. Occasionally, however, a new writer has material to offer worth, at any rate, our study; and Willibald Franke, the German art critic, is justified of his volume which describes some twenty years' experiments with his "psychograph", a combination of ouija and planchette.[4] It is a significant book. His theory, as a non-spiritualist, is also significant.

Briefly, his theory, modestly offered neither as psychologist nor expert, is that *all* automatic communications are the deliveries of the subconscious minds of the sitters; they are dreams (of light or deep slumber) because the "subconscious prefers the dream-form"; their substance, often verified later as to names, dates, events, is provided by one or other of the sitters, since "every individual carries his ancestors within himself"; and the guiding spirit, or control, is a dominant trait in someone present, dramatising itself. The voluminous literature of the subject, of which he admits (and obviously) complete ignorance, bears him out. The unreality of the dream-like puppets who "communicate" at séances, in automatic writing, etc., is undeniable. They remain the puppets in a poorly conceived, weakly imagined play.

The sittings here described cover twenty years, with frequent change of sitters. "The phenomena we are studying closely resemble the dreams of our deepest slumber, which rarely penetrate to consciousness . . . The communications, like dreams, may be regarded as manifestations of the subconscious mind, formant in a waking state . . . elicited in a purely automatic way by a force proceeding from the sympathetic nervous system, and this force is generated by the co-operation of the various persons taking part and guiding the psychograph." The clue to the whole mystery is to be found in the sympathetic nervous system, the pressure of the cerebral brain being removed. "Questions are the means of setting free in the subconscious mind associated ideas to which its *creative* phantasy gives a definite direction." Why, in other words, drag in discarnate spirits? It is in the resemblance between the "communications" and dreams that the author gains our attention. In the suggestion that every man "carries his own ancestors within him" he rivets it. Here is an instructive and promising line of enquiry, to say the least.

It is not wholly new. That the subconscious mind "prefers the dream-form" is known to every artist. Gustave Geley (*From the Unconscious to the Conscious*, 1921) emphasised it. The amazing content of the subconscious mind is too well known, from numerous books, to bear repetition. Its dramatising powers, similarly, have been drummed into us. Hélène Smith, remembering a former life on Mars, invented its language, grammar, script and signs on the spur of the moment, all based on her own native language, French (*From India to the Planet Mars*. Prof. Flournoy, 1900). The theory is well documented, but it is left to our author to submit this valuable material as something of a climax which sums up the whole question. "It is not my object to gain adherents," he mentions modestly, "or to force my view on anybody, but merely to offer this body of honest experiment to psychologists who may use it"—as we may hope they will.

The sittings, sixty in number, are reported verbatim, with the author's comments. The majority of the "communications" are utterances of persons who could be authenticated in history, many of them hundreds of years "dead", their existence not even consciously known to any of the sitters. The author's children obtained astonishingly accurate results. The sitters were constantly changing, wholly inexperienced. It was always question and answer. Yet there was nothing that could be traced eventually to the subconscious or ancestral knowledge of one of the sitters. "We are therefore tempted to assume that a man's personality does to a certain extent persist in his descendants, and that his mental gifts are imparted, just as the primal biological cell, ever dividing and multiplying, yet transmits a portion of its own substance to far-off descendants." The ancestral, even racial memories of the sitters are drawn upon. "Man is a product of his ancestors, and every man has received some of the mental endowments of his many forefathers."

Certain communications state: "I am in you. I am merely your thought . . . You live on in the generations to come. Beget offspring and you will live forever . . . I am always near you and I guide your brain . . . " utterances which, without any straining of their meaning can be interpreted as indicating that a mental heritage received from some ancestor gives the tendency to a man's thought and feelings. On one occasion a girl who used the psychograph owend—through a great-grandfather—French blood in her veins. Though full of German patriotic feeling, she had a certain French bias. At this sitting the talk was mixed with French phrases: "a proof of hereditary transmission of psychic impressions and intellectual gifts and of their unconscious expression by the psychograph". Record No. 20, again, showing two persons talking, begins in pure German. A Tyrolean song is then asked for and instantly the Tyrolean dialect is substituted.

Present among the sitters was a Tyrolean poet . . . On yet another occasion, Fetzer, a Rhine robber of 1487, unknown to all, yet later verified, announced: "There is not a man living who is not injured, and not a man dies who does not bear to his grave a hurt given by the hand of a friend." The author's wife, present at the sitting, had read and admired *Timon of Athens* many years before. The passage thus roughly reproduced occurs in Act I, Sc. 2. The woman's subconscious mind gave up its dead.

"In dream," says the author, "we carry on conversations with several persons, and single individuals oppose each other with arguments and counter-arguments, struggling to convince one another, while all this proceeds from the dreamer himself. He *creates* a dream in which various persons are made to appear in the conversation dreamed of, and the standpoint of first one, then another, is assumed . . . Things are done not in the least desired by the dreamer, often indeed causing him anxiety and mental stress. If the unconscious manifests itself thus in dreams, there is no reason for assuming it would be otherwise in these communications." The dialogues of planchette are the dialogues between the questions of the conscious mind and the answers of the subconscious mind using the phantasy of the dream-form. Many of the sittings, indeed, read like the "wild dream of a disturbed sleep, sometimes of light, sometimes of deep slumber." Logic is ruled out. Subconscious processes are dream-processes. "In a dream," says Bergson, "we become no doubt indifferent to logic, but not incapable of logic. There are dreams when we reason with correctness and even with subtlety . . . Generally the logic of a dream is feeble enough, and often resembles a mere parody of logic."

As we read the verbatim account of these sixty séances, it is difficult not to agree with the author's contention

164

that we are dealing with "communications" whose bewildering and irrational character betrays their affinity with dreams. The parody of logic is ever present; there is amazing accuracy, yet there are amazing errors too. The discrepancies are worthy of note . . . "another argument in favour of the idea that communications, like dreams, are a play of phantasy in the subconscious mind". That sudden introduction of the Tyrolean dialect, again, is true to the dream-process when "through some external influence, either of touch or sound, the dream-creating phantasy is immediately effected, accepts the impression and weaves it into vision". The night-time of the body, said Iamablichus, is the day-time of the soul.

The individual, therefore, this writer considers as a multiple being, a multiple unity, a *Vieleinigkeit*, as the German calls it, and psychology supports him. The guide, control, familiar, genie—it has numerous titles—"should be regarded as that force in the soul of man which is to some extent the dominating influence in the inherited spiritual currents of the subconscious". The individual, through this submerged reason, is in touch with racial and planetary memories of all that has ever existed. "When we consider the existence of such a stored-up treasure," says the author, "we are forced to the conclusion that a large proportion of man's life-task must be regarded as merely a kind of rendition of that which exists in the subconscious." Dr. Gustave Geley declared, similarly, that Nature exists for the purpose of rendering the Unconscious conscious.

Dream phantasy is apparent in all automatic revelations. Swedenborg held discourse with Luther and Melanchthon. They lived, this latter pair, in a house allotted to them, which resembled their earthly dwelling in every respect. They busied themselves with pursuits which had occupied their earthly life, Melanchthon writing day after day, sheet upon sheet of absolutely aimless dissertations upon "Justification by Faith alone". "How childish," says the author, "to imagine the after-life of the soul continued in surroundings which correspond in every way with the ideas and conditions of corporeal existence. How strictly limited to the measure of Swedenborg's own cognition is the philosophy here evolved! A proof that it all originated within himself alone." What a tremendous triumph for science, he cries, if it could find a way in which this dormant treasure could be made easily available, instead of being left to chance and the chaos resulting upon chance!

A confession by the famous Mrs. Piper is significant here, though not mentioned in the volume under review.[5] This famous medium, in an interview published in the *New York Herald* so long ago as 1901 (quoted by A. J. Philpott in his revealing book, *The Quest for Dean Bridgman Connor*, 1915), stated categorically, "I have never heard anything being said by myself while in a trance state, which might not have been latent in (1) my own mind; (2) in the mind of a sitter; (3) in the mind of the person who was trying to get communications with someone in another state of existence, or some companion present with such person, or (4) in the mind of some absent person alive somewhere else in the world."

The author ends on a note of admirable common-sense:

> Everything that exists is in accordance with reason and therefore suited to its end. If it were one of the aims of cosmogony to establish intercourse with the spirit-world, such intercourse would occur frequently, and reveal something loftier than trivialities.

III.

"The stars won't bear thinking about," declares the Rajah in *The Green Goddess*, "and as a spectacle they're monotonous." He expresses the unimaginative view. Charles Nordmann, of the Paris Observatory, is more imaginative. "Astronomy," he says, "is the least short-sighted of human disciplines. It tends to make man more modest, more agnostic, less assertive, dogmatic, and sectarian. It holds us dizzily over those precipices where the physical and the metaphysical touch. The Attraction of the Unknown is full of bitter sweetness."[6]

In this stimulating book he writes, "not to instruct or amuse, but to produce thoughts and even dreams, if I can." The lure of the unknown is in his blood; he luckily has technique and a telescope; he is the man of science as poet. His imaginative mind discusses only the most recent star secrets as revealed by the spectroscope on the "little dust particle we call the Earth". The wonder and beauty of what he tells us are staggering, to the layman often incredible, but they are never fanciful. Awe and reverence go hand in hand. He quotes with approval the master mathematician, Henri Poincaré: "People ask the gods to prove their existence by miracles. But the eternal miracle is that there are no miracles." The cosmos is not governed by caprice. The most impressive fact that emerges from a consideration of the heavens is the sense of law and order, as of divine Intelligence, which pervades the whole gigantic business.

Mr. Nordmann's recent book, *Einstein and the Universe* (1921; trans. 1922) went into numerous editions in France and was among the best-sellers. The present volume should share its fate. "Most thinking people," he writes in a preface touched with humour, "aspire at times to escape from the military or monetary controversies which characterise our 'idealist' times . . . Novels? These glittering fictions are often modelled too narrowly upon meagre human realities. Love has been surrounded with poetry by Art, and with ecstasy by Nature . . . Yet we must have other enthusiasms . . . Fairy Tales? These are nothing compared to the telephone, x-rays, stellar spectroscopy, etc. . . . . Arts and Letters? Past ages have equalled them . . . The world's political and social changes? Ten thousand years these have moved in the same vicious circle. There remain the sciences—in particular the most finished of them, the most disinterested: the stars. Stars are adorable because they resemble those chimæras for which hopeless love seeks in vain." Our nostalgia for the infinite, refusing to be stifled, finds in the stars a remunerative field for exploration.

Leaving our familiar "dust particle", the Earth, we leave also the friendly blue air (its colour due merely to our thin skin of atmosphere) and plunge through the true sky, which is black, "a deep black of eternal mourning". Accosting the planets in passing, we race onwards to the Sun, "whose singular magnetic and electric influences, like a sort of telepathy, make us tremble at its slightest spasm", and thence take our upward rush to those "strange ant-heaps, called clusters, and finally to the vertiginous spiral nebulæ".

We spend a week-end on the moon, however, *en route*, for no astronomer can ever leave the moon alone. This trumpery little satellite holds too many mysteries among her mountains, 24,000 feet in height and her craters 21,000 feet in depth.[7] Her strange acceleration, for one thing, has now been fully explained. It is only a few seconds of arc per century, one second of arc being less than the 800,000th part of a right angle, but that she should be apparently slowing down was a disquieting puzzle. The solution of the mystery lies in the fact that the Earth herself is the laggard, turning less and less quickly on her own axis. And this is due partly to the friction of the present oceans on the ocean floor, and partly to the intense friction of the viscous and more fluid portions of the Earth's interior. These drag at her. The moon does not turn more slowly, but the sidereal day is increasing. The strange "patches of vegetation" noticed by Professor Pickering, are also mentioned and explained away. They appear just after sunrise, spread over enormous acres, then disappear in a few minutes again. They were observed in the bottom of the steep craters. They are due to "the refraction of the sun's rays by myriads of crystals with sharp edges".

Mars detains us for a moment or two, with its double hint of artificial canals and possibly inhabitants. The canals are an optical illusion, a mirage, due to the use of low-power telescopes which tend to make dots look like lines. Through a high-power telescope there are no lines at all. Mr. Nordmann is very positive on the subject. He is less positive with regard to life on the planet, where, in any case, there is less oxygen than on the top of Mount Everest. After discussing the possibility that life-germs reach the Earth first upon some meteorite or other body after a journey of countless *light-years*, he admits his readiness to believe that life may exist elsewhere. "This does not mean that thinking organisms only exist on the Earth," he says. "I am even inclined to be convinced of the contrary . . . Yet nothing has yet proved that life exists anywhere but here . . . Is it not wiser perhaps," he asks, "to consider organised life as a protoplasmic accident, as rare in space as it is in time?"

We land next on the Sun—only 93,000,000 miles away, whereas some of the stars are 400,000 *light-years* away—light, of course, travelling 186,000 miles a second. We have no space for detail here, but the way the Sun's constant loss of heat is restored as interest—by contraction. Its diameter grows five hundred feet less annually, and this contraction engenders enough heat to replace what is poured out so prodigally. The process may continue some eight million years before we notice any difference. It has been held until recently that by the time our planets fall into the Sun (their eventual fate), the Sun would be cold. How radium has changed this prophecy. The planets will take their final rush and plunge into the Sun still hot. "Life will be volatilised in the grand crematorium, the Sun," states Mr. Nordmann almost with enthusiasm.

In his contemplation of the appallingly distant "island universes" we cannot follow him here, nor listen to his fascinating description of the new method of measuring a star's diameter. Betelgeuse, we know from this discovery, is as large as the orbit of Mars round the Sun—which reminds us of the Rajah's comment that the stars won't bear thinking about. The author closes his volume, at any rate, on a practical note about something nearer home: the use of the tides to help our daily work along. The tides provide an extremely powerful machine with the movement of an alternating piston. "When humanity emerges from its ignorance," he hopes and believes, "it will utilise the thousands of millions of horse-power. Then, no more under the necessity of devouring each other in order to live, people will occupy themselves with science, art, etc . . . " The French government, he informs us, has already inaugurated this Golden Age by appointing a commission to attack the problem at certain points on the coast.

7 December 1923;
11 and 25 January 1924.

Notes

[1] The full title is *The Wonderland of the Eastern Congo* (1922).

[2] Edgar Rice Burroughs would later incorporate the Leopard Society into his novel *Tarzan and the Leopard Men* (1935), serialised in *Blue Book*, August 1932 to January 1933.

[3] It seems that none has been seen or captured since and it remains an enigma.

[4] *Voices from Another World* (1923) by F. Gurtis (pseudonym for Willibald Franke), translated by Lilian A. Clare.

[5] Leonora Piper (1857-1950) was a famous American medium who was subject to extensive research by the Society for Psychical Research and in particular by William James. Many believed her abilities at the time but in later years researchers came to the conclusion that she was a very skilled fraud.

[6] Quoted from *The Kingdom of the Heavens, Some Star Secrets* (1923) by Charles Nordmann, translated by E. E. Fournier d'Albe.

[7] The tallest mountain on the moon is generally recognised to be Mons Huygens at 18,000 feet, though the Selenium Summit plateau rises to over 35,000 feet, but that is on the far side of the moon and thus not observable from Earth. The deepest crater on the moon is the South Pole—Aitken basin which has a depth up to 27,000 feet deep, but that is also on the far side. The deepest crater on the near side would seem to be Hercules G which has a depth of around 22,600 feet.

Queer Stories

When I came into this quiet little studio my head was so packed with queer stories that I hardly knew which I was going to tell you first. But a glance at the microphone at once stopped that sort of nonsense. Its mechanical little round face has something formidable, almost monstrous, that insists upon order. It makes me think of voodoo and African idols. So I've quickly decided on a few stories, each of distinctive type, which I hope may interest you. And, with that idol staring at me, I'll begin with one about magic—Indian magic.

Yogi

A young Englishman was spending a week's leave on a bit of shooting. He had with him a *shikari*, and one evening at sunset they pitched camp on a low cliff of mud beside a river. Below them was a strip of foreshore with scrub and bushes. It was a lonely part of the country. While the servant prepared the evening meal behind him, the Englishman stood idly cleaning his gun and smoking, when something moving down the river caught his eye. The river was broad, with very little current, it lay golden in the sunset blaze, and the floating object puzzled him at first, till he examined it with his glasses and saw that it was a body. Lying on its back, it moved slowly with the sluggish current and something about the face that had at first puzzled him proved, on closer examination, to be a bunch of coarse grass—stuffed into the open mouth. The *shikari*, after using the glasses in his turn, explained the grass with which the mouth was filled—a local superstition according to which evil spirits were prevented taking possession of the body. Death, he declared, had evidently been quite recent. It was the body of a strapping young native in good preservation.

There was nothing particularly thrilling in the sight, and the Englishman went on cleaning his gun, while his *shikari* went on cooking the supper just behind him—when a moment later the man uttered a curious sound. He had left his fire and was staring over the cliff to the shore. There was a touch of awe on his face. He was pointing down to the strip of foreshore. And as the Englishman followed his gaze he saw an old native, dressed in a loin-cloth, emerging from the bushes. He was very old; he was also very emaciated.

"See! A Holy Man!" whispered the *shikari* under his breath, and dropped upon his knees. His whole attitude became one of awe and reverence. "Watch," he whispered. They watched together.

The aged figure, some forty feet below on the shore, moved slowly to the edge of the water and began making curious signs and gestures over it—slow, sweeping movements of the arms and hands—and obviously towards the body. "He is bringing it in; he needs it," whispered the *shikari* in his own tongue. "Watch!"

Whether due to natural currents and eddies of the water, or not, the body came slowly in, nearer and nearer, till at last it lay on the sand at the old man's feet. They saw him stoop, then, and draw it from the river, dragging it after him some dozen yards till he disappeared behind the bushes. The Englishman, watching the proceedings through his glasses, saw that it was the body of a young man in perfect preservation.

"Now wait," whispered the servant. "We see something more."

The Englishman waited, his eyes fixed upon the clump of bushes. He was an understanding sort of fellow. He didn't curse and swear because the dinner was burning away behind him. He respected the awe and veneration his servant showed. The man was trembling.

He waited. Ten minutes later there was a movement in the clump. The young man walked out. He walked away. The Englishman with his glasses followed him till he melted away in the sunset haze. It was the body that had floated in the river.

Half-an-hour later, they climbed down the cliff and there, behind the clump, lay the worn-out, cast-off body of the old man in the loin-cloth.

Blank Cartridges

In case the last story left an unpleasant taste, here's a more cheerful one about a man who slept in a haunted room and got a shock he didn't expect. He was a hard-boiled sort of fellow, who wasn't a scrap frightened by the supernatural. If a ghost had walked up to his bed he would merely have said, "Wrong room, I think," and turned over to sleep again. No pose. Really felt like that.

But on this particular occasion he had his suspicions. He rather thought there might be a practical joke. So he gave his companions fair warning. He told them he would take a pistol to bed and if he saw a figure or anything, he would shoot. He meant it too. "I shall count first: one— two—three," he said, "then shoot." He showed them the pistol, too.

How he contrived this particular pistol is beyond me—for it fired duck shot—fine pellets that could sting all right, but not necessarily kill. He used it for rats, I believe. Anyhow, that's what his pistol was like, and what *he* was like.

He went to bed and in due course fell asleep, with the loaded pistol under his pillow. In the night he suddenly woke up with a feeling that someone was in the room. At the same moment he saw a dim figure in the darkness at the foot of his bed. There was no time to turn the light on. Out came the pistol instead. He pointed it. He shouted, "I count three—and then fire."

The dim grey figure did not move. It made no sound.

He counted in a loud voice: "One, two, three"—and fired at the legs. The figure moved an arm slightly like making a catch, and the duck shot was tossed back and fell all over his chest and shoulders in a shower.

The man aimed again, but the pistol shook a little, for the hand that held it also shook a little: "One—two—three"—he counted again, loudly—and his voice wasn't so steady either—and fired. There was the same movement of the shadowy arm. The shot was flung back over him in a shower. It fell and trickled down his chest and shoulders, against his skin inside his pyjamas.

The third time he gave no warning at all. That is, he did shout "one, two, three", but he fired simultaneously. He aimed higher, too. He aimed at the heart. But hand and pistol wobbled so violently that it's doubtful if he could have hit a haystack. And this time the figure again made the gesture of a catch, then stretched out a long shadowy arm across the bed into his very face and dropped, not a shower of duck shot, but a single bullet, plop, upon his bare neck. He felt its weight. He felt it slide off his shoulder and heard the thump as it landed beside him on the mattress. He also heard the figure give a low chuckling laugh.

175

The complete blackness that followed—well, he denies vehemently that he lost consciousness, even for a second. Within five minutes, at any rate, and this time with the light turned on full, he caught one of his companions in a grey dressing-gown, loose bullets in one pocket and a quantity of duck-shot in the other—and gave him what he thoroughly deserved.

He always declared that he knew by the weight of the pistol in the hand that the shot had been abstracted and the cartridges were blank.

Homicidal Dream

The next story, whatever may be thought of the last one, is certainly true. It happened a good many years ago.

A young girl had an extremely vivid and unpleasant dream, a nightmare, in which a man strangled her in bed. She woke in terror. The man's face, as he leaned over her, was terribly clear. It was a face she would recognise anywhere, and could never forget. She told the dream to her parents, her brothers and sisters, her cousins and her aunts, who all combined to argue it out of her and make her forget it. But she could never forget it.

It was perhaps a year later she went with her elder brother on a week-end visit to a house they did not know. While driving from the station it suddenly came to her with dreadful conviction that this was the house of her dream. It was an utterly unreasonable conviction, nothing to support it. But it was so strong that she told her brother she could not face it. She must get out.

Her brother, though he thought it was hysteria, had the greatest difficulty in the world to make her change her mind. He was kind and patient and, in the end, he persuaded her by promising that he would never once leave her. He would stick closer than a brother. If she recognised the face of her dream, either among guests or servants, he would get her out of the house, no matter what it meant. He swore it.

They found at least a dozen other guests when they arrived, and more came later. The brother kept his word faithfully. He was always within reach. He looked over her bedroom, with the small dressing-room out of it. He kept asking her if she had seen the face. No, she had not, but she was frightened still. Nothing could shake her conviction that this was the house of her dream. He didn't oppose or argue; he was clever about it. He said, "Well, you may be right, but it won't happen *this* visit. It's another visit. And we can meet that by never coming again."

He realized that she was genuinely scared, whether hysteria or not, and he met her halfway, as it were. As far as possible he kept to her, always within reach. He even made some plausible excuse to leave the dinner table with the ladies so as to be on hand in case she suddenly saw the face she dreaded.

But she did not see the face. It was a cheery party, too. They danced and amused themselves. It was quite hilarious. The fact that the electric light plant broke down added to the spontaneous fun. They finished dinner by candlelight, played bridge, etc. It was after midnight when the party broke up and made for bed. Carrying a candle apiece, as in Victorian days, all went upstairs. But candlelight, of course, does introduce another atmosphere. She was on edge. "Goodnights" followed, and the brother went with his sister to her room.

"Now, look here," he said. "You haven't seen the face, have you?"

"No," she said, "I haven't. But all the same, I'm frightened." And she actually *was* trembling. The gaiety she had forced all the evening was gone.

"Well, I'll come in and search your room," he said, "then you can lock your door. You'll be quite safe then. My room is just opposite anyhow."

They went in and put their candles down. It was a large room. At the far end was a dressing-room and, as the door of this dressing room also opened into the corridor, her brother said he would first go and lock it on the outside before he made his search.

He wasn't gone thirty seconds when he heard a wild shriek of terror. He was back in a moment to see his sister leaning against the wall in a state of collapse while, at the far end by the window, stood a man. He had evidently just come out of the dressing-room, for its door stood open. The man was in the livery of the house, a sort of under-footman apparently. The brother asked him what he was doing there. But the man had a perfectly legitimate explanation. He had been fastening the windows in the further room. It was his job. He spoke quietly and respectfully, and walked out. There was really nothing unusual about it at all. But the girl was almost speechless with terror.

"That's the face I dreamed about," she said.

Her brother managed things quickly and quietly. He gave her his own room and made a bed for himself on the sofa. No one had heard the shriek, luckily. Although he thought that the coincidence of the footman in the room made his sister believe it was her dream-face, he did not say so. And nothing happened in the night, while it was a simple matter next day to wangle some excuse for leaving. The girl refused point-blank to pass another night in the house. And who can blame her?

It was a week later when the brother met his host again in the club and heard that an unpleasant thing had cropped up in the household just after the week-end party. One of the men servants, an under-footman, had suddenly developed acute homicidal mania, and was already certified. "Thank God," said his host, "it didn't happen when you were all there!"

The brother, now more than interested, went to the trouble of verifying that the homicidal maniac and the man who had been in his sister's room were one and the same. But he never let his sister know—nor, of course, could he ever prove that the face in the dream was the face of the homicidal footman.

Evidence in Camera

Now, there's just time to squeeze in another. The face of the Idol opposite me looks hungry still. Like some insatiable Moloch, or Oliver Twist asking for one more mouthful. So here's a very short one that should satisfy its appetite about a man who suffered from a most distressing delusion— he believed he was being followed and haunted by some dreadful figure with an appalling face. In everything else he was as sane as you or I. But this one horrible apparition, showing itself at intervals, and always just behind him, ruined his life as well as threatened his mental sanity. No one else ever saw it. For that matter he longed to believe it was subjective merely, a creation of his own imagination. Oh, he was sane enough about it all, but terrified as well. It had gone on for years. He had been through every imaginable treatment without success until a couple of doctors, who were interested in his case, hit upon an ingenious plan.

They asked his permission to take a photograph of him at the moment he saw the awful thing over his shoulder. And he agreed. It involved waiting patiently for a day or two, but at last the opportunity came—one afternoon, in the garden. The sufferer gave a sudden cry. He turned white as chalk. He gave a terrified look over his shoulder.

The horrible apparition, he exclaimed, was there. Well the camera, always at hand, was ready instantly. The photograph was taken. It was developed within half-an-hour. But the two doctors, in the dark-room, exchanged puzzled looks. They agreed it was impossible to let their patient see the plate. They told him it was bad. He never saw it.

28 August 1934.

Sources

"Looking Back at Christmas" was first published in *Leader Magazine* (25 December 1948).

"I Speak for Myself" was broadcast on BBC Far Eastern Service on 3 December 1949. This is its first appearance in print.

"How I Became Interested in Ghosts" was broadcast on BBC television on 13 October 1951. This is its first appearance in print.

"The Midnight Hour" was first published in *The Queen* (24 November 1948).

"Minor Memories" was broadcast on BBC Third Programme on 8 September 1949. This is its first appearance in print.

"My Strangest Christmas" was first published in *Radio Times* (24 December 1948).

"Little People and Co." was broadcast on BBC Third Programme on 25 December 1948. This is its first appearance in print.

"The Birth of an Idea" was broadcast as "The Genesis of Ideas" on BBC Home Service on 3 March 1948; it was published as "The Birth of an Idea" in *London Mystery Magazine* #6 (Oct./Nov. 1950). An earlier but radically different version was published as "The Genesis of Ideas" in *The Writer* (February 1937), reprinted in *Fantasy Commentator* #34 (Winter 1984).

"Our Former Lives" was first published in *Prediction* (May 1947).

"The Fire Body" was first published in *The North American Review* (September 1931).

"Passport to the Next Dimension" was first published in *Prediction* (March 1948).

"Adventures in Thought-Transference" was first published in *Prediction* (December 1949).

"Oddities" was broadcast on BBC Home Service on 31 August 1948; it was first published in *The Listener* (9 September 1948). The central section from "Oddities" has been excised to avoid repetition; it was replaced with an extract from "Some Remarkable Dreams", which was first published in *The Strand Magazine* (February 1933).

"Gooseflesh" was first broadcast in the series "Books and Authors" on BBC Light Programme on 31 January 1948. This is its first appearance in print.

"Along Came a Spider" was first broadcast on the BBC Home Service on 10 June 1950 under the title "Spiders and Such"; it was first published as "Along Came a Spider" in *London Mystery Magazine* #8 (February/March 1951).

Sources

"The Fear of Heights" was first broadcast on the BBC Home Service on 29 October 1947; it was first published in *The Listener* (6 November 1947).

"Superstition and the Magic 'Curse' " was first published in *The Daily Express* (9 April 1923).

"The Psychology of Places" was first published in *The Westminster Gazette* (30 April 1910).

"Dreams and Fairies" was first published in the special Christmas number of *The Bookman* (December 1929).

"Explorers' Ghost Stories" was first published in *The Occult Review* (July 1925).

"The Lure of the Unknown" was first published in three parts in *Time and Tide*: 7 December 1923, 11 January and 25 January 1924.

"Queer Stories" was broadcast on the BBC National Programme on 28 August 1934; it was first published in *The Listener* (12 September 1934).

Acknowledgements

I would like to thank and remember the help provided by Patsy Ainley, who brought so much of Blackwood's life alive; Barbara Lindsay, who solved a major mystery which opened so many doors; and my dear friend Michael Pointon, who somehow kept pointing me in the right direction. This book is dedicated to their memory.

About the Author

Algernon Blackwood (1869-1951)—journalist, novelist, broadcaster—is best remembered for his occult detective John Silence and, in particular, two terrifying tales of otherworldly encounters: "The Willows" and "The Wendigo". The intensity of Blackwood's stories often arose from personal experiences: his days struggling to survive in the hell of 1890s New York, his travels down the Danube, across the Caucasus, into the depths of Egypt, or the remote mountain passes in Switzerland—all fed his fascination with Nature.

About the Editor

Mike Ashley has been collecting, researching and writing for almost sixty years and has over thirty thousand books and magazines. His passion for research began when his father used to tell him about stories he had read but could not always remember the title or author, and that sent young Ashley off to the library. He's still doing it, and it has led to over 130 books, mostly anthologies and collections, but also reference works ranging from *Who's Who in Horror & Fantasy Fiction* to the biography of Algernon Blackwood, *Starlight Man*, and books about British Kings and Queens, King Arthur, and even the Seven Wonders of the World.

SWAN RIVER PRESS

Founded in 2003, Swan River Press is an independent publishing company, based in Dublin, Ireland, dedicated to gothic, supernatural, and fantastic literature. We specialise in limited edition hardbacks, publishing fiction from around the world with an emphasis on Ireland's contributions to the genre.

www.swanriverpress.ie

"Handsome, beautifully made volumes . . . altogether irresistible."

– Michael Dirda, *Washington Post*

"It [is] often down to small, independent, specialist presses to keep the candle of horror fiction flickering . . . "

– Darryl Jones, *Irish Times*

"Swan River Press has emerged as one of the most inspiring new presses over the past decade. Not only are the books beautifully presented and professionally produced, but they aspire consistently to high literary quality and originality, ranging from current writers of supernatural/weird fiction to rare or forgotten works by departed authors."

– Peter Bell, *Ghosts & Scholars*

SELECTED POEMS

George William Russell (A.E.)

Published in September 1935, just two months after his death, A.E wrote of *Selected Poems*, "If I should be remembered I would like it to be for the verses in this book. They are my choice out of the poetry I have written." A.E.'s life-long friend and sometimes rival, W. B. Yeats, observed that his poetry expresses "something that lies beyond the range of expression", and that he has within him "the vast and vague extravagance that lies at the bottom of the Celtic heart." To commemorate the 150th anniversary of A.E.'s birth, Swan River Press is pleased to reissue this career-spanning collection of poems from a key artist of the Celtic Revival. This volume includes selections from *The Earth Breath*, *Voices of the Stones*, *The House of the Titans*, and others, introducing a new generation to Ireland's foremost mystical poet.

"Yet, bathed in gloom too long, we might
Forget how we imagined light."

– The Twilight of Earth

THE SATYR & OTHER TALES

Stephen J. Clark

In the final throes of the Blitz, Austin Osman Spare is the only salvation for Marlene, an artist escaping a traumatic past. Wandering Southwark's ruins she encounters Paddy Hughes, a fugitive of another kind. Falling under Marlene's spell Hughes agrees to seek out her lost mentor, the man she calls The Satyr. Yet Marlene's past will not rest as the mysterious Doctor Charnock pursues them, trying to capture the patient she'd once caged. *The Satyr* is a tale inspired by the life and ethos of sorcerer and artist Austin Osman Spare.

Another three novellas of occult enchantment follow: a bookseller discovers that his late wife knew the Devil, in the Carpathian Mountains refugees shelter in a museum devoted to a forgotten author, and in Prague a portraitist must paint a countess whose appearance is never the same twice.

*"This book will adorn your shelves, where it will be
at ease in shadowy converse with your copies of À Rebours,
The Picture of Dorian Gray, The Great God Pan."*

– Mark Valentine

*"Clark's subtle prose, vivid and disturbing imagery,
and the concepts he weaves into his stories make
them irresistible to those whose senses
have been jaded by more common fare."*

– *Black Static*

THE HOUSE ON
THE BORDERLAND

William Hope Hodgson

An exiled recluse, an ancient abode in the remote west of Ireland, nightly attacks by malevolent swine-things from a nearby pit, and cosmic vistas beyond time and space. *The House on the Borderland* has been praised by China Miéville, Terry Pratchett, and Clark Ashton Smith, while H. P. Lovecraft wrote, "Few can equal [Hodgson] in adumbrating the nearness of nameless forces and monstrous besieging entities through casual hints and significant details, or in conveying feelings of the spectral and abnormal."

"Almost from the moment that you hear the title," observes Alan Moore, "you are infected by the novel's weird charisma. Knock and enter at your own liability." *The House on the Borderland* remains one of Hodgson's most celebrated works. This new edition features an introduction by Alan Moore, an afterword by Iain Sinclair, and illustrations by John Coulthart.

*"A summit of Cosmic horror.
Scary, disturbing and magical."*

– Guillermo del Toro

*"Swan River Press has produced the best version ever.
There is no need for any other."*

– *Dead Reckonings*

Printed in the USA
CPSIA information can be obtained
at www.ICGtesting.com
CBHW020236050924
13971CB00023B/158